TEACHING GRAPHIC NOVELS IN THE CLASSROOM

GRADES 7–12

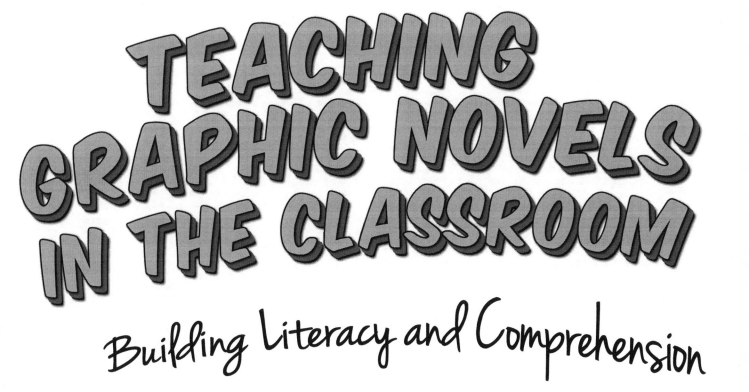

Teaching Graphic Novels in the Classroom

Building Literacy and Comprehension

RYAN J. NOVAK

PRUFROCK PRESS INC.
WACO, TEXAS

DEDICATION

For my wife, Lindsey, for loving me, supporting me, and always encouraging me to work harder and be my best. I'm a lucky guy.

For my grandfather, Carley Jones, for buying me *Amazing Spider-Man* #235 and *Marvel Tales* #4 on a trip to the grocery store, which was not only how I learned to read, but where my love of graphic literature was born.

Library of Congress Cataloging-in-Publication Data

Novak, Ryan J., 1978-
  Teaching graphic novels in the classroom : building literacy and comprehension / by Ryan J. Novak.
    pages cm
  ISBN 978-1-61821-107-1 (pbk.)
  1. Graphic novels in education. 2. Graphic novels--Study and teaching (Secondary) 3. Language
arts (Secondary) I. Title.
  LB1044.9.C59N68 2013
  371.33--dc23
                              2013025372

Edited by Rachel Taliaferro

Cover and layout design by Raquel Trevino
Ilustrations by Zachary Hamby unless otherwise noted.

ISBN-13: 978-1-61821-107-1

Printed in the United States of America.

At the time of this book's publication, all facts and figures cited are the most current available.
All telephone numbers, addresses, and websites URLs are accurate and active. All publications,
organizations, websites, and other resources exist as described in the book, and all have been verified.
The author and Prufrock Press Inc. make no warranty or guarantee concerning the information and
materials given out by organizations or content found at websites, and we are not responsible for any
changes that occur after this book's publication. If you find an error, please contact Prufrock Press Inc.

Prufrock Press Inc.
P.O. Box 8813
Waco, TX 76714-8813
Phone: (800) 998-2208
Fax: (800) 240-0333
http://www.prufrock.com

TABLE OF CONTENTS

PREFACE

Welcome to *Teaching Graphic Novels in the Classroom: Building Literacy and Comprehension*, a textbook that presents a wide array of graphic novels as they deserve to be presented: not just as "big comic books," but as *literature* to be read and discussed. Obviously, as graphic literature has grown more popular in recent years, the sheer volume of novels is enormous. I have chosen one to two novels for each chapter that I feel are the best representation of the medium in that genre. I have designed the book to educate all readers, regardless of whether they have or have not previously read any graphic literature. Please feel free to contact me with comments and suggestions.

Ryan J. Novak
ryanjnovak@gmail.com

ACKNOWLEDGEMENTS

This book was born from the excellent memory of my friend and mentor, Zachary Hamby, who—a year ago—remembered a brief conversation we had when I spotted Jeff Smith's *Bone* (a personal favorite of mine) in his classroom library when I was his student teacher. It was Zak who suggested that I submit a proposal for this textbook. My gratitude to him cannot be measured, nor can my debt to him ever be repaid.

In my moments of doubt during the writing of this book, it was the encouragement of my colleagues, Melissa Everett, Karen Price, and Dianne Richart, that helped me. I would also like to recognize the members of the comic book club that I sponsored, all of whom helped me test many of the activities that are included in this book: Tia, Chris, Hannah, Daniel, Matt, Keagan, Nathaniel, and Trevor. Thank you for keeping me inspired through your enthusiasm and support. You've done well, Avengers.

I give special thanks to my friend Chris Stewart, who would make the trip to Book Barn with me to pick up comics so many times in high school; Josh Roberts, my friend and comic guru, who has always been quick with recommendations and is a bottomless comic encyclopedia (thanks for giving me such a great discount, too). Finally, I'd like to thank my family: my mom, Sue Novak; my dad, Jim Novak; my stepmom, Jayne Novak; my siblings, Jennifer, Shannon, Luke, and Christian, for their endless love and encouragement.

TEACHER'S GUIDE

I was 4 years old the first time I saw a comic book. On a trip to the grocery store with my grandfather, I saw a spinning metal rack of them at the front of one of the aisles and was immediately drawn to the cover art. I recognized *Superman* because my parents showed me the movie, which was one of my early obsessions. Like a lot of children my age, this resulted in me tying my security blanket around neck like a cape and jumping off my bed, proclaiming that wherever I was speeding off to in my imagination was a job "for Superman!"

Comic books, though, were new to me. Up until that point, Superman inhabited the same world as The Muppets and Darth Vader, as he was solely the property of movies. That he had an entire life in a medium that was completely foreign and amazing to me was a revelation. That day, my grandfather bought for me two *Spider-Man* comics after making me promise that I not share the information with my grandmother, who would deem it "immature" and "silly."

Although I could read at the time, *Spider-Man* proved to be a much greater challenge to me than the simple children's storybooks that I was used to, and the word balloons were far more complicated than the short exchanges between Charlie Brown and Linus Van Pelt. I was left staring at the pictures and attempting to piece together the story. With my grandfather's aid, I was able to learn how to read a comic book, how to follow which word balloon belonged to whom, and how to follow the action.

1

TEACHING STRATEGIES FOR GRAPHIC LITERATURE

Many students may not have previously been exposed to reading graphic novels or comic books and may run into the same difficulties that I had when I first encountered one. There are several methods a teacher may employ to help learners improve their understanding and appreciation of the medium. All of these methods can be differentiated for different reading levels.

Sequential Storytelling: Make a copy of a classic nine-panel page of a graphic novel and cut the page into individual panels. Working in small groups of two to three students, have the students figure out the sequencing of the page and put the panels back together in their proper order.

Without Words: Take a page of a graphic novel that contains at least six panels (nine for a greater challenge) and remove all of the dialogue and action descriptions. Present the "wordless" page to your students and ask that they attempt to follow the story without the dialogue and explain what is happening in the scene. This activity is very helpful in teaching students to learn to follow the action of a story, especially when teaching a book that does not have words to begin with, such as Shawn Tan's (2007) *The Arrival.*

Predicting: Similar to the "Without Words" strategy above, take a page of a book and remove the dialogue from every other panel of art. Have students predict what was said in the blank panels that would lead to what happens in the following panel, which will still have the dialogue and action descriptions. Just as above, use at least a six-panel page.

Dialogue: Again take a six-to-nine-panel story and remove the dialogue and action descriptions, but this time have the students try to not only figure out the action, but also fill in the dialogue from each character. Then show the students the panel with the original dialogue so they may see how close their predicitons came to the actual dialogue and if they maintained the narrative of the story.

Pass It Along: Taking the above strategy, put students in small groups of three to five. Have one student write the dialogue for the first panel and pass the page along to the next student, who fills in the second panel. Have the students keep passing it along until the page has been filled in entirely.

Summarizing: Use this as a cumulative activity once the students have become proficient at reading graphic literature. Start with having them summarize one page at a time.

Reader's Theater: Reader's theater plays are very effective at helping students interact with the material. By having them convert portions of a graphic novel into reader's theater plays, students' comprehension of the material may be enhanced.

What's important to remember is that, at their core, graphic novels are still novels. Although the above strategies may prove to be very helpful in teaching the material, you are free to use any other methods you would use for teaching a traditional novel.

Throughout the book, you will see essential questions at the end of different sections of each novel and at the conclusion of each novel. The questions can be used as you wish, whether it is solely for comprehension of the story or as quizzes to accompany the reading. All of the sidebar activities are meant to be used as enhancement, as prereading understanding for each novel, or to expand upon specific themes, motifs, and symbols during reading. The timelines presented at the start of each chapter are merely suggestions based on what has worked for me in the past—you are free to create your own timeline according to the needs and pace of your classroom. In Appendix A and Appendix B at the end of the book, you'll find suggested reading and film guides. These novels and films can be used to enhance teaching, as their own stand-alone lessons, or be left out completely. Appendix C includes a suggested scoring rubric for the project in Chapter 9. For teachers who aren't familiar with the medium, this rubric should help guide them in judging students' work.

Finally, I should note that some of the graphic novels in this book may include content that can be unsuitable for younger readers. I recommend previewing each book before giving it to students. The graphic novels covered in this book are:

- *The Dark Knight Returns* by Frank Miller;
- *Watchmen* by Alan Moore;
- *The Sandman: Preludes and Nocturnes* by Neil Gaiman;
- *V for Vendetta* by Alan Moore;
- *Metropolis* by Osamu Tezuka;
- *A Contract With God* by Will Eisner;
- *The League of Extraordinary Gentlemen* by Alan Moore;
- *Maus* by Art Spiegelman;
- *Ghost World* by Daniel Clowes; and
- *American Born Chinese* by Gene Luen Yang.

WHY STUDY GRAPHIC LITERATURE?

Sequential art, whether you call it a comic book or a graphic novel, has long reflected our culture. Although they have not always been recognized for doing so, comic creators have found myriad ways to comment on society. For example, although known primarily for his arch-nemesis, Lex Luthor, and for the World War II-era covers that featured the Man of Steel punching Hitler or Hirohito, Superman began as a social crusader. In his early adventures, Superman forced a greedy munitions maker to join the Army so that he would see the terrifying side of the war being fought for his benefit. In another story, he battles a cruel mine owner who doesn't care for the safety or well-being of his mine workers. Other stories focused on Superman dealing with a slumlord who refused to update his tenement buildings that had fallen into disrepair.

Similarly, in the 1960s, in response to the fantastic worlds that the DC Comics characters inhabited, Marvel Comics had its characters lived in the real world.

Spider-Man lives at home with his aunt and has money problems; the Fantastic Four, although a team of superheroes, are a dysfunctional family at their core; and the superhuman X-Men face prejudice in the world by protecting people who often ostracize and hate them.

Long believed to be the province of children, comic books have over the years displayed a social conscience while reflecting the sometimes ugly parts of our society. As comic readers grew up, the major publishers started focusing on more mature storylines that their now-older readers would find interesting. In the late 1960s and early 1970s, comic books tackled the growing concern over drugs. In *Spider-Man*, Peter Parker's longtime friend and son of the Green Goblin, Harry Osborn, was discovered to be a methamphetamine addict. In DC Comics, Green Arrow's sidekick, Speedy, turned out to be addicted to heroin.

In teaching various novels, regardless of grade level, I have found that students have an anxiety about reading. Although there are students who love to read and are always excited when they know that the class will consist of reading and discussing a novel together, there are a great many students who have the immediate reaction of "What? Do we *have* to?" It is many of those same students who are apprehensive about reading who are also quick to discuss in great depth their favorite TV shows and movies. Given the popularity of movies based on comic books, such as Christopher Nolan's series of Batman films or Joss Whedon's *The Avengers* (Fiege & Whedon, 2012), I've used graphic literature in my classroom more and more to draw the students' interest from the movies to the literature.

With technology playing an increasing role in their lives, students need visual stimulation to be a part of their education. Students are increasingly visual learners and are taken in by the art as much as the story. The art allows them to invest themselves more emotionally with the story and increases not only their interest in reading, but their visual learning skills as well. The emotional connection—to the art, story, or characters—is a key to visual literacy. The various layers to graphic literature that go beyond the text alone allow the students to analyze the story on different levels. They are able to analyze the story beyond what they would encounter in traditional literature. Using graphic literature to teach visual literacy will deepen the connection that students have with traditional texts and allow them to be visual readers, even when the text is not accompanied by visuals. This ability increases their enjoyment and proficiency as readers.

By learning with graphic literature, students not only learn how to interpret how art enhances the level of storytelling, but their ability to interpret messages that are sent through various everyday forms of art and visual media is increased. With this awareness comes an enhanced ability to be more discerning and even skeptical of all forms of visual media. Being able to interpret the connection between visuals and texts and the emotional responses that both can elicit will make students more informed viewers who are less susceptible to manipulation through advertising.

CHAPTER 1

THE HISTORY OF COMIC BOOKS AND GRAPHIC LITERATURE

ORIGINS

Comic books find their origin in ancient cave paintings and the narrative woodcuttings of the medieval broadsheet, which often featured caricatures of public figures and narratives about executions. Once the printing press was born, these broadsheets were collected together in what was an early magazine prototype.

There has been much debate over the years as to what the first graphic novel was. The mid-to-late 1800s saw the publication of the first books to feature sequential art. Rodolphe Toffler's *The Adventures of Obadiah Oldbuck* was published in 1842, which first appeared in a humor magazine called *Brother Jonathan* and told the story of a boy through captioned cartoons. In 1895 came the publication of Richard Outcault's *The Yellow Kid*, which, like Obadiah, was first a comic strip syndicated in newspapers.

However, the closest relatives of comic books were early pulp magazines. Contrary to magazines that were printed on glossy paper, pulp magazines gained their name because of the cheap wood pulp paper on which they were printed. Following in the footsteps of 19th-century dime novels, pulp magazines saw the height of their popularity from the early 1900s through the end of World War II. Their relation to comic books, aside from the paper stock, comes from the regular feature of full-length, illustrated stories about characters like The Shadow (an early radio hit of the 1940s, like Superman) and Doc Savage. Rising costs of publication, along with competition from comic books and radio plays that featured similar stories, led to the end of pulps shortly after World War II.

Roots in Classic Mythology

One of the functions of storytelling is to understand the world around us. The Greeks and Romans used the tales of powerful gods and goddesses as a way to understand the world. Fortunes, both good and bad, were attributed to the fickle nature of those who lived upon Mount Olympus. Just as the Greeks once did, we too use tales of gods and goddesses as one way understand the world around us. The only difference is that our gods and goddesses wear tights and have superpowers. Superheroes function as a modern mythology, and the characters often reflect different parts of our culture and help explain so much about ourselves.

The original incarnation of The Flash was based in appearance on Hermes of Greek mythology. With wings on both his shoes and cap, Flash was a strong visual representation of Zeus' son, the messenger god.

Parallels can be drawn between Superman and Hercules, as both characters have unbelievable strength. Hercules is as powerful as the gods, if not more so, but is not allowed to live on Mount Olympus, just as Superman lives in a world that is not his own. Relying more on cunning and intelligence than on any supernatural powers, Batman can be seen as a modern-day counterpart to the Trojan War hero Odysseus. Bruce Banner's alter ego, the furious Hulk, is in many ways like Ares, the Greek god of war, as both are brutal and merciless.

Although parallels can be drawn between several superheroes and the gods and goddesses of classic mythology, no one character draws as heavily on those stories as that of Wonder Woman. Created by Harvard psychologist William Moulton Marston, who saw a lack of positive role models in comic books for young girls, the character was the daughter of Hippolita, the queen of the Amazons, who created her from a ball of clay. Marston, who is also credited with the invention of the lie detector, gave Wonder Woman a magic lasso that forces people to tell the truth. When the Amazons sought to select the most powerful warrior to stop a plot by Ares to end the world, it was

Compare

Read a few stories about Hermes, such as the "Theft of Apollo's Cattle" (available at http://www.hemlockandhawthorn.wordpress.com/2013/03/01/apollos-cattle), and research online the original incarnation of The Flash. What parallels do you see between the two characters, besides their appearance?

Wonder Woman who was chosen. Ares is not the only classic mythological character to make regular appearances in the Wonder Woman mythos—Circe, the sorceress whom Odysseus encountered during his long journey home, has been a regular in Wonder Woman comics as well.

Although many other parallels can be drawn between Greek mythology and comic book superheroes, the most important parallel is that both serve as a way to examine our own society. Just like their mythological counterparts, superheroes serve as the ultimate in human possibility. They are morally good and mentally and physically superior. However, they are also instilled, just as the gods were, with the same failings as humans. Within them lie the same hopes, dreams, and failures that we find within ourselves.

While boys had Superman, among other popular heroes, young girls did not have a strong female role model. Wonder Woman was designed to be that role model for young girls. Do you believe that she was successful? Why or why not?

GOLDEN AGE: 1938–1955

The first comic book to be published in the format that is still used to this day came in 1934 with the publication of *Funnies on Parade* by the Connecticut company Easter Color. The format was chosen because the size of the newspaper page allowed for four pages of material to be printed to the page and then folded twice. It was not sold anywhere but was instead available for people who mailed in coupons for Proctor & Gamble products.

However, the dawn of what is regarded as the Golden Age of comic books is usually recognized as the publication of *Action Comics* #1, which marked the first appearance of Superman. Prior to his debut, National Allied Publishing (later to be rechristened as DC Comics after its successful title, *Detective Comics*) had published detective and western comics. When the company needed a lead feature for the debut issue of *Action Comics*, they gambled on Superman.

Previously rejected by multiple newspapers, writer Sheldon Mayer saved the Man of Steel from a reject pile and took it to editor Vin Sullivan. The immediate success of *Superman* led to a shift in focus by publishers from detective and western stories to superhero stories. *Superman* was followed closely by the first appearance of Batman in *Detective Comics* #27 in May of 1939. Within the next 2 years, DC Comics published the first stories to feature Aquaman, The Flash, Green Lantern, Hawkman, and Wonder Woman. Timely Comics, later to be known as Marvel Comics, produced their first superhero stories in *Captain America*, *The Human Torch*, and *Sub-Mariner*. Outside of DC and Timely, Fawcett Comics had success with *Captain Marvel*, which outsold even *Superman*; Quality Comics, later owned by DC, had *Plastic Man* and Will Eisner's syndicated *The Spirit*.

Following the end of World War II, more and more comics began to feature atomic-based stories and characters, including the Atomic Thunderbolt. The era also saw a decline in popularity of superhero stories as the focus began to spread to funny animal characters, crime, horror, romance, war, and western comics. The exact end of the Golden Age of comics is debated as coming with the cancelation of Captain Marvel, Plastic Man, or DC's Justice Society of America.

Creator Profile

Jerry Siegel and Joe Shuster

Jerry Siegel was born to Lithuanian-Jewish immigrant parents in Cleveland, OH, in 1914. At the age of 16, he befriended Joe Shuster when the pair both attended Glenville High School. Shuster was born to Romanian-Jewish immigrants in Toronto, Ontario. His family moved to Cleveland when he was 9 years old. In high school, the pair worked together on their school paper, *The Torch*, with Siegel writing stories, including a Tarzan parody, which Shuster would illustrate.

Following high school, Siegel and Shuster broke into the fledgling comic book industry with the publication of their first stories in Malcolm Wheeler-Nicholson's *New Fun*, which featured characters such as the swashbuckling and Musketeer-like character, Henri Duval, and the supernatural crime fighter, Doctor Occult.

The pair also created a telepathic supervillain called Superman in their own self-published fanzine (a fan-magazine) called *Science Fiction*. The lone appearance of the evil incarnation of the iconic character came in issue #3, before the duo decided to reconsider the character.

Their reimagined version of the character was eventually published by DC Comics, which bought the rights to arguably the most recognizable character in comic history for a whopping $130 and a contract to produce more material for the company. At the end of their 10-year contract, Siegel and Shuster attempted to sue the company over rights to the now immensely popular character. Siegel later returned to DC in 1959 but severed his relationship permanently with the publisher when he again attempted to sue the company in 1967. Starting in 1976, the duo was credited permanently as the creators of Superman in every issue and was granted a $20,000 per year pension.

Joe Shuster passed away in 1992, followed by Jerry Siegel in 1996. Over the years, the Siegel estate has continued to have legal issues with DC Comics, including a lawsuit filed in 2006 over the creation of Superboy, which Siegel had first proposed to DC prior to World War II. After Siegel returned from serving in the war, he found that DC had published the character without giving him credit. Just as their most famous creation, Superman, has come to stand for hope and morality in an increasingly turbulent world, the duo of Siegel and Shuster have come to represent the battle for creator rights in the comic industry.

The Superman Era

In his origin, the most recognizable character in comic book history was born as a bald, telepathic madman. Based on German philosopher Friedrich Nietzsche's concept of the "Übermensch," "The Superman" was a villain bent on world domination. The character's lone appearance came in issue #3 of Jerry Siegel's own fanzine, *Science Fiction*, in 1933.

Realizing the limitations of casting the ultimate human being as a villain, Siegel and co-creator Joe Shuster decided to recast the character as a crusader for good. As part of the duo's new vision, Superman would no longer be born of Earth but would instead be the last son of a distant, dying planet. Drawing both from the religious iconography of Moses floating through the reeds and the Christ-like notion of a child being sent to Earth to one day be its ultimate savior, Superman was a hero from another world.

Visually, Superman was based on actor Douglas Fairbanks, and his glasses-wearing alter ego, Clark Kent, was based on Harold Lloyd. The name "Clark Kent" was taken from a combination of Clark Gable and Kent Taylor. His iconic costume drew its inspiration from circus strongman outfits and the space-aged look of characters like Flash Gordon. Siegel and Shuster initially offered it to Consolidated Book Publishing, who rejected it. It was also rejected by National Allied Publishing, who had previously published the duo's character, Slam Bradly, in the first issue of *Detective Comics* (the same comic that later published the first appearance of Batman). The company eventually took a chance on Superman and published his first appearance in the June issue of *Action Comics*.

Originally, Superman was a rough and very aggressive superhero who was more of a social crusader than superhero. Before the creation of supervillains Lex Luthor and Braniac, Superman took on mobsters, slumlords, lynch mobs, and wife beaters, and the character did not have the strict moral code that he's recognized for today. As his rogues' gallery of villains grew over the years, later writers instilled the character with an idealism and morality that is typified by his quest to protect "truth, justice, and the American way." His modern perception as being unwilling to vary even slightly from a path of righteousness has been regularly attributed to the "small town values" that were instilled in him by his Earth parents, Jonathan and Martha Kent, who raised him on a farm in the fictional town of Smallville, KS.

Many of Superman's classic elements did not come by way of the comic books. The character initially could not fly but simply would leap great distances. His ability to fly was first introduced in the 1940s radio serial, *The Adventures of Superman*, with each flight preceded by the phrase "Up, up, and away!" Although the radio show changed certain elements of his story, such as his quick maturation during his flight from Krypton and his arrival on Earth as fully grown, the show also introduced kryptonite (pieces of matter from his home planet) as the only substance that could stop the otherwise unstoppable Man of Steel, which became an enduring part of his mythology. The radio show also introduced eager photographer, Jimmy Olsen, who joined Clark Kent; Lois Lane, Superman's girl-friend and later wife; and publisher Perry White at *The Daily Planet*. His 1950 film appearance, in *Atom Man vs. Superman* (Katzman & Bennet, 1950), saw the introduction of the evil scientist, Luthor (not yet Lex Luthor).

Today, after success in comics, movies, and video games, Superman has transcended his own success and reached the point of being recognized as a cultural icon. His name invokes images of patriotism, as well as hope for a better day. His symbolic S-shield has become synonymous with bravery and inner strength. When actor Christopher Reeve was paralyzed in a horse-riding accident, he used the Superman symbol from his most iconic role for his Christopher Reeve Foundation, which funded research into cures for paralysis.

Superman: Religious Icon?

Over the years, the life of the last son of Krypton has been viewed as a religious allegory. Created by the children of Jewish immigrants by way of Lithuania and Romania, the character has had strong ties to the Jewish community. Comic book publishers regularly hired Jews because prejudice at the time kept them from employment in many other more "legitimate" occupations. In their early days, Siegel and Shuster submitted work under the name Bernard J. Keaton to protect themselves from rejection based on their heritage.

Although Superman has become an icon to many people and a symbol of strength, Siegel and Shuster, who were themselves often oppressed, created Superman as a crusader for the oppressed. As one of the first superheroes, Superman was the first to make use of the secret identity, that of the mild-mannered reporter, Clark Kent. It has been often theorized since the character's inception that Superman is a metaphor for the hopes and dreams of a Jewish immigrant—or any immigrant in general—in America. That someone foreign could arrive and not only be accepted for who he is but become symbolic of the fantastic possibilities of his adopted home gave people hope. Just as it happened with so many Jewish immigrants as they passed through Ellis Island, Superman was given a new name upon his arrival when he was adopted by the Kents. Just as Siegel and Shuster once used a fake name to sound less Jewish, baby Kal-El of Krypton would become "Clark Kent" to sound more normal in his new home. Superman represented the ideal we all wish to achieve, while Clark Kent lived his life revealing the awkwardness that we all tried to keep hidden away in our quest to be accepted and loved.

As America entered World War II, the news of the caped crusader and his religious overtones and that of the heritage of his creators reached all the way to the Third Reich. The Nazi Minister of Propaganda, Joseph Goebbels, denounced Superman as a "Jew." The character and its creators were ripped apart in the German-controlled press, which mocked a character created by a Jew for being called "Superman."

The attention Superman received brought along with it a new view of his origin story, which closely resembled the story of Moses. In the Biblical story of Moses, the Israelites in Egypt were threatened with the murder of their male offspring. Moses' mother, Jochebed, sought to save the life of her infant son and placed him in a reed basket and sent him adrift down the Nile River. Similarly, Jor-El, faced with the destruction of his entire planet, chose to save the life of his infant son by placing him a small craft and sending him out into space.

Moses is discovered by the Pharaoh's daughter, Batya, just as Kal-El is discovered by a farm couple, the Kents. Both young men are raised in foreign countries and initially hide their identity, with Clark Kent hiding his alien self and Moses masking his Israeli origin for many years.

Despite the Jewish origins of the characters, many Christians have found parallels between Superman and Jesus Christ. In the comics, baby Kal-El is sent to Earth by his father and grows up to be a savior to the people of his new home, just as God sent his only son to Earth as a savior to the people. Superman's arrival on Earth is seen by his ship appearing like a shooting star in the night sky over a Kansas farm field, just as Jesus' birth was heralded by shepherds in a field by a star in the night sky. Clark, like Jesus in Nazareth, is raised in a small town, Smallville. In the story of Jesus, he is raised by an adoptive father on Earth, who is a carpenter by trade. Similarly, Clark is raised by a farmer, another manual labor job. In the original story, Clark's parents were even named Joseph and Mary, which was changed by the publisher to Jonathan and Martha.

Throughout comics and films, Superman is often portrayed hovering above Earth listening carefully for those who are in need of his aid, which has been viewed as a metaphor for Christ listening to people's prayers at night. Superman's arch-enemy, Lex Luthor (whose name even recalls that of Lucifer's), is bitter and envious of Superman's powers and the adoration that he receives, just as Lucifer is of God's power. It is not until he is older that Clark comes to understand his origins and the trials that lie ahead for him, just as Christ did not understand his faith until he was much older. Like Christ before him, Superman eventually sacrifices himself only to be resurrected.

Whether you see the religious parallels to Moses, Christ, both, or neither, these allegorical notions of the character speak to the immense strength that readers are able to interpret and use to explore who they are and what they believe in.

DISCUSS

Why might Superman be identified so closely with two major religions?

WRITE

Besides Superman, what other superhero character do you feel has religious significance? Why?

How Comics Won the War for the Allies

What would you do with unlimited power? Would you solve the world's problems? During the rise in the popularity of superheroes, World War II broke out, and even before America entered the war following the Pearl Harbor attack, comic books were addressing the growing war in Europe and Asia.

Created by Joe Simon and Jack Kirby, Captain America (originally named "Super American" but renamed by Simon because of the prevalence of "Supers" in comics) was a purely political character because his creators morally opposed the actions of the Nazi Party. Captain America made his debut when the first issue of the comic was released in December of 1940, a full year before Pearl Harbor. He made his debut in glorious fashion, too, landing a punch square on Adolf Hitler's jaw on the cover of the issue.

Despite selling almost a million copies, there were people who took issue with Captain Steve Rogers (Captain America's real name) and everything that he stood for. Simon and Kirby even received death threats from people showing up at the Timely Comics offices looking for the pair. Throughout his World War II-era run, Captain America and his sidekick, Buddy, regularly fought alongside the Allied forces against the Axis Powers.

Although Captain America was a soldier, albeit with a soldier imbued with superpowers, his powers were limited. However, his patriotic counterpart at National Allied Publishing, Superman, could do anything. But despite being created as a social crusader who fought very real villains, like corrupt politicians and slumlords, Superman stayed out of the war. The covers of his comics, *Action Comics* and *Superman*, indicated otherwise, though. Starting with the September 1941 issue, the Man of Steel was shown walking alongside a sailor and a soldier, despite America not yet having entered the war. Throughout the remainder of the war, Superman covers regularly showed him fighting alongside the Allies, destroying enemy tanks or swimming angrily towards a Nazi U-Boat, the latter of which was viewed through a periscope by two panicked Nazi officers.

The content of the issues rarely ever touched on the war, even after America got involved. Not wanting to ignore the war entirely, Superman's creators had Clark Kent attempt to join the army. During his physical, he accidentally uses his X-ray vision, reads the eye chart in the next room, fails his eye exam, and is classified as a 4-F, making him undraftable. With a convenient excuse as to why he can't enter the military and affect the outcome of the war, Clark returns to work as a reporter at *The Daily Planet* and covers the war. He makes periodic returns to Europe, helping train the troops in a June 1943 issue, declaring them to be super soldiers.

In order to not trivialize the very real and continuing war effort, many authors chose not to have superheroes become directly involved with the war— even though, ostensibly, a superhero would be capable of easily resolving a war.

To publish a story in which Superman wipes out the Nazi menace and ends the Holocaust would have been disrespectful to the people engaged in or affected by the war. One November 1943 issue of *Superman* hinted at the author's feelings about having a superhero get physically involved in the war effort. The issue, called "The King of Comic Books," involved a comic creator whose creation, "Geezer," regularly beat up the Axis powers, which led the Nazis to kidnap the artist and threaten to kill him before Superman arrives dressed as Geezer to rescue him at the last minute. Following his rescue, Superman cautioned the man about the dangers of being so rash and arrogant.

Superman did find one way to aid the Allied forces, however. The military was drafting several thousand men every year who were expected to be able to operate heavy machinery, but many of them had little education, some even being illiterate. In order help teach them to read, the newly rechristened DC Comics produced Superman comics with simplified dialogue, and the issues were distributed to the G.I.'s.

Would it have been a disservice to the soldiers during World War II to have issues of comic books in which superheroes ended the war on their own?

Comic Books: Threat to Society?

Throughout the history of comic books, fans have heatedly debated who is the greatest villain in the history's medium. The Joker? Lex Luthor? Or is it the real-life Frederic Wertham?

Frederic Wertham was a German-born psychiatrist who nearly killed every superhero in existence, a feat thought impossible by Dr. Doom, Magneto, and Braniac. Following the adage "the pen is mightier than the sword," Dr. Wertham (1954) published a book called *Seduction of the Innocent*. Today, it is familiar territory for violence in our culture—especially among teenagers and adolescents—to be blamed on violent video games, like *Grand Theft Auto* or violent movies like *The Terminator*. Similarly, Dr. Wertham felt that the rise of juvenile delinquency could be blamed on comic books.

Although Wertham distributed the blame evenly between superheroes and crime comics, his assertions about superheroes were especially ludicrous. It was his opinion that comic books contained graphic depictions of drug use, sex, violence, and other "adult themes" that were corrupting the minds of the young. Even though William Moulton Marston created her as a strong role model for young girls, Dr. Wertham interpreted Wonder Woman's strength to be manly and concluded that she was a lesbian. She was not the only character Wertham interpreted as homosexual—Batman and Robin, a young boy being raised by a single man, were interpreted as having a homosexual-pedophilic relationship.

Wertham's book led to Senate hearings about the influence of comic books on juvenile delinquency. The United States Senate Subcommittee on Juvenile Delinquency was formed in 1953, and in 1954, it focused on comic books, par-

ticularly ones that focused on horror and crime and contained violence. The hearings, which took place on April 21, April 22, and June 4 of 1954, resulted effectively in the death of E.C. Comics because of its focus on crime and horror comics and in the creation of the Comic Code Authority (Senate Committee on the Judiciary, 1954). The Comic Code Authority prohibited the disrespect of authority, especially "policemen, judges, government officials, and respected institutions" (General Standards—Part A). Excessive violence was forbidden, as were the use of the words "terror" or "horror" (General Standards—Part B). There could be no visual depictions of any lurid, gruesome, or unsavory behavior. Any form of lewd behavior, such as sex, seduction, rape, sadism, or masochism was also prohibited. Although Dr. Wertham did not entirely kill comic books, he did manage to beat them to the point of near-submission.

SILVER AGE: 1956–1970

Following the publication of *Seduction of the Innocent* and the creation of the Comic Code Authority at the end of the Golden Age, comic books went through a dark period that saw a drop in readers. The Silver Age began with DC Comics' publication of *Showcase* #4, which introduced the new Flash. Although the old Flash and the new Flash shared essentially the same powers, with only their origins and costumes being different, the birth of the updated Flash marked something new for DC Comics. For the first time, a hero other than Superman, Batman, and Wonder Woman was selling. The arrival of the new Flash opened the door for updated versions of The Atom, Green Lantern, and Hawkman.

In the shift from the Golden Age to the Silver Age of comics, the most noticeable change was to more science-fiction-based superpowers. With the exception of Superman, most Golden Age heroes had magical powers. The Silver Age, born in an era obsessed with science-fiction films, saw a noticeable transition in character origins to fit the trend.

The chief rival to DC Comics—the "esteemed competition"—was the former Timely Comics, now known as Marvel Comics. When DC Comics published its new superhero team book, *Justice League*, Marvel publisher, Martin Goodman—who was notorious for following trends—remarked to his writer, Stan Lee, that he should create a similar book, which resulted in the publication of *The Fantastic Four* in November 1961. Its success led to the launch of now-famous characters Hulk in *Incredible Hulk* #1 in May of 1962 and Spider-Man in *Amazing Fantasy* #15 in August of the same year. The success of Marvel soon came to force DC Comics into an artistic drought. Marvel's take on superheroes was fresh and new, while DC was still marketing its comics exclusively to children.

The end of the Silver Age came with two events. The first was a new creative team on Green Lantern, who took the book in a more serious direction that came to exemplify the Bronze Age. The second event was Steve Rogers abandoning the mantle of his alter ego Captain America after the Watergate-themed storyline in which Rogers becomes disgusted by government corruption.

Creator Profile

Stan Lee

Born Stanley Martin Lieber to Jewish-Romanian parents in New York in 1922, Stan Lee is known as one of the most legendary, recognizable, and enduring personalities. Following World War II, Lee found work in the fledgling world of comic books for Timely Comics. Eventually moving on to writing, Lee—along with artists such as Jack Kirby, Bill Everett, and Steve Ditko—would go on to create *The Fantastic Four*, *The Hulk*, *Spider-Man*, *Iron Man*, *Daredevil*, and the *X-Men*.

One of Lee's greatest innovations was to create a sense of community among comic readers and creators. He added a letter section at the end of every issue called "Stan's Soapbox," in which he would answer fan's questions, talk about the characters and stories, and promote upcoming Marvel comics. In addition, he also was the first creator to not only share credit with the artists, but with the inker and letterer at the introduction of every character.

As a creator, Lee had a unique system of writing in which he would come up with a general outline for every issue instead of a firm script. This method, known as the "Marvel Method," allowed the artist to have more input in the story and character development. When the artist would turn in the finished art, Lee would go through the art and write all of the captions and dialogue.

Predating any other comics touching on modern social issues, Stan Lee was the first creator who chose to eschew the Comic Code Authority with three issues of *The Amazing Spider-Man* published in the late spring of 1971. At the request of the U.S. Department of Health, Education, and Welfare, Lee wrote a story, "Green Goblin Reborn," in which Peter Parker's (Spider-Man) best friend, Harry Osborn, becomes addicted to pills. Despite the very clear antidrug message of the story, the Comic Code Authority refused to allow the comics to be printed with their seal because they depicted drug use, a prohibited topic. Realizing the importance of the story and the message it would send to younger readers warning them of the dangers of drug use, Lee decided to publish the issues without the Comic Code Authority seal. His bold move led to the eventual rewriting of the Comic Code to allow for negative depictions of drug use.

These days, Stan Lee is a goodwill ambassador for comic books. He still continues to write, as well as create content in other media. He is very active in charity work through his own Stan Lee Foundation, which focuses on literacy and the arts. He is also an occasional actor and can be seen as a chess player being interviewed on the news at the end of *The Avengers* (Fiege & Whedon, 2012) and as a very oblivious librarian at Peter Parker's high school who continues to shelve books while listening to music, even as Spider-Man and the Lizard tear apart the school in *The Amazing Spider-Man* (Arad, Tolmach, Ziskin, & Webb, 2012).

Superheroes in the Real World

One of the greatest differences between DC and Marvel Comics is the worlds in which they exist. DC Comics characters live in fictional cities, although debatably based on real-world cities, such as Gotham, Metropolis, Keystone City, and Coast City. When Stan Lee began to craft the Marvel Universe, he looked no further than his home in New York City. Daredevil, Spider-Man, the Fantastic Four, and the Punisher, among others, all called New York home.

In addition to basing the world on real locations, Marvel published the first comics to give characters real-world problems; contrary to that, DC Comics characters always seemed to have personal lives that were free from financial troubles or other personal woes. The real-world struggles and failures have come to define Marvel Comics throughout the ages. For example, Spider-Man was left to the care of his aunt and uncle after his parents disappeared. After the death of his uncle, Peter and his Aunt May often experienced financial struggles.

The ultimate nuclear family, The Fantastic Four, was a group of superheroes who would fight crime and then bicker amongst themselves upon their return. Their powers are also metaphors for who they are as people. Reed Richards, the super stretchable Mr. Fantastic, is an overworked scientist who often stretches himself thin through his work. Sue Storm, later Sue Richards, often feels inferior and her complex is exemplified by her power of invisibility. Johnny Storm's hot-headed and impulsive nature is perfectly characterized by becoming a man who literally catches on fire, The Human Torch. Ben Grimm (one of the first Jewish superheroes), always a stand-out for his monstrous size and the reaction he receives for being so large, becomes the orange rock monster, The Thing.

BRONZE AGE: 1971–1985

Although the Golden and Silver Age of comics were marked by very singular events—the debuts of Superman and the new Flash respectively—the Bronze Age did not have any particular story or debut that heralded the dawning of a new age. The Bronze Age is distinguished by its move toward darker storylines. In 1971, both Marvel and DC Comics had storylines dealing with drug abuse. As mentioned in the creator profile, Marvel writer, Stan Lee, published a story arc at the request of the U.S. Department of Health, Education, and Welfare that revealed Peter Parker's best friend, Harry Osborn, to be a drug addict. Not to be outdone, DC produced a *Green Lantern/Green Arrow* story called "Snowbirds Don't Fly" that dealt with the revelation that Green Lantern's sidekick, Speedy, was addicted to heroin. Marvel also had an eight-issue story arc in Iron Man, "Demon in a Bottle," that addressed Tony Stark's alcoholism.

Substance abuse problems were not the only controversial issue to make an appearance in comics—racism was also frequently addressed. Although Marvel's Black Panther and DC's Falcon were for many years the only well-known black superheroes, the 1970s saw a rise in the number of African American superheroes and villains. Marvel's Luke Cage became the first African American character to star in his own monthly title in June of 1972, with Black Panther getting his own title in 1973. Storm became the first female African American character when she joined the X-Men. Restrictions on vampires, zombies, and monsters by the CCA were loosened, which led to the half-vampire African American, Blade, receiving his own title. DC Comics had its first Black character in new Green Lantern Corps member John Stewart, who even briefly replaced Hal Jordan as the main Green Lantern. The character Cyborg joined, and later led, the Teen Titans.

Like its onset, the end of the Bronze Age did not come with a specific event. The generally accepted timeframe for the end of the era coincided with DC's "Crisis on Infinite Earths" event, which saw years of continuity being streamlined and several characters dying, including the Silver Age Flash, who was replaced by his nephew, Wally West. Writer Alan Moore lovingly said goodbye to classic Superman, who was to later be revitalized by John Byrne in the two-part story, "Whatever Happened to the Man of Tomorrow?"

Creator Profile

Jack Kirby

With a career that dates back to the creation of Captain America, Jack Kirby is one of comics' unsung heroes. Like many early comic creators, Kirby was of Jewish descent, being born Jacob Kurtzberg to Austrian-Jewish immigrants in 1917.

Following his success with Captain America for Timely Comics, Kirby and Joe Simon briefly had their own imprint, Mainline Publications, from 1954 to 1956, which published primarily war comics. After the company folded, Kirby went to work for DC Comics, working on titles such as *Challengers of the Unknown* and *Green Arrow*.

It was in 1958, when Kirby went to the newly rechristened Marvel Comics, that he found his greatest success. Working on anthology titles like *Strange Tales*, *Tales to Astonish*, and *Tales of Suspense*, he also freelanced for *Archie Comics*. Kirby came to define not only the Marvel style of comics but the style of comics for decades to come, starting with the publication of *The Fantastic Four*.

The team of Jack Kirby and Stan Lee created *The Hulk*, *Iron Man*, *Silver Surfer*, and *Thor*, among other titles. The duo also created the mutant superhero team, The X-Men, and the first major black superhero, The Black Panther.

For the remainder of his career, Kirby worked again for DC Comics, as well as Marvel. He passed away from heart failure in 1994. Although his name is not as well known as that of his longtime creative partner, Stan Lee, his mark on the art style in comics is indelible.

MODERN AGE: 1986–TODAY

If DC Comics ended the Bronze Age with "Crisis on Infinite Earths," it also kick-started the Modern Age with the publication of two landmark series (both explored in Chapter 2), Frank Miller's (1997) *The Dark Knight Returns* and Alan Moore's (1995) *Watchmen*, both of which dealt with the mortality of superheroes. As many of our heroes were each placed in an existential crisis, the era became marked by the antihero, such as Miller's take on Batman and Image Comics' Spawn.

Independent comics and specialty lines from major publishers became popular during this era. More subversive works, such as Alan Moore's revamping of DC's *Swamp Thing*, led to the company launching Vertigo Comics, which would specialize in comics that were told outside of the superhero mainstream. The publisher would become synonymous with titles like Neil Gaiman's (2012b) *Sandman* and others like *Hellblazer*, *Preacher*, *100 Bullets*, *Fables*, and *Y: The Last Man*.

Creator's rights played a major role in the creation of Image Comics, the first viable imprint to give serious competition to the two major publishers. Founded by a group of Marvel Comics writers and artists, Image Comics was built around creator-owned titles. Working for the two major publishers, the creation of any new character would automatically give the company the rights to that character. Image Comics, however, allowed for the rights to all content created for the company to remain with the creator. It made Image an appealing new imprint and gave it great success throughout the 1990s.

The modern era of comics has seen mainstream acceptance of comic books. Starting in 1989 with director Tim Burton's Frank Miller-inspired *Batman*, Hollywood took an even greater interest in developing comic properties for the big screen. Over the last two decades, *The X-Men*, *Spider-Man*, *Iron Man*, *Thor*, *Captain America*, *The Avengers*, *300*, and the previously thought unfilmable *Watchmen* have all become huge hits on the silver screen.

Graphic literature has long reflected the modern world we live in, not just in style but in its depiction of society. Why is it important that it reflect our culture, even when it means reflecting on the darker aspects of it, such as drug use?

Alternative Comics

Although both Marvel and DC struggled to get stories published that served as cautionary tales about drug abuse, there was an underground movement in comics that saw the publication of stories that depicted strong sexual content and drug abuse, like R. Crumb's *Zap!* and *Cheech Wizard*. For years, alternative comics were unfairly associated with subversive or taboo topics, instead of simply being a platform for emerging writers and artists to present stories that were not in some way superhero tales.

By the late 1970s, Dave Sims began self-publishing his title *Cerebus* under his own Aardvark-Vanheim imprint. The comic ran for 300 issues, an astounding number for a title that did not have distribution by any of the major publishers. In 1980, Art Spiegelman of *Maus* fame and his wife, Françoise Mouly, produced the anthology *Raw*, a large format comic that showcased work that was intended to be viewed as art. The following year saw the return of R. Crumb with his own magazine, *Weirdo*.

The first great success of alternative comics was Mirage Studios' *Teenage Mutant Ninja Turtles* from Kevin Eastman and Peter Laird, which was not only an edgy and influential title but later became a hit cartoon and was developed into a series of movies.

A friend of *Cerebus* creator Dave Sims, Jeff Smith (2004) produced another long-running and wildly successful independent title with his series, *Bone*. A finite series since its inception, *Bone* was not only incredibly successful but was so while managing to appeal to both children and adults. Printed in black-and-white for the entirety of its run, the entire series has been republished in color and has taken its rightful place as one of the most popular graphic novels of all time.

Within the last few decades, several publishers have emerged that specialize in publishing of alternative titles, such as Fantagraphics Books, Drawn and Quarterly, and Top Shelf Productions. These companies have been responsible for the release of several major works, including Daniel Clowes' (2001) *Ghost World* Craig Thompson's (2003) *Blankets*, and Chris Ware's (2003) *Jimmy Corrigan: The Smartest Kid on Earth*.

Rise of Graphic Novels

The term "graphic novel" is a point of contention for many writers and artists. Legendary creator Alan Moore has dismissed the term as being nothing more than a marketing term and that "comic book" is fine by him. When asked if there was a meaningful difference between a comic book and a graphic novel, *Sandman* creator Neil Gaiman said, "No, there's no meaningful difference. For some reason the term 'big thick collected or original comic published in book form' has never really caught on, while 'Graphic Novel' did" (Gaimain, 2004, para. 23). Some have mockingly pointed out that the difference between a comic book and a graphic novel can be found in the binding.

The difference isn't in the binding but in the intended scope of the story. A graphic novel is a novel told through words and pictures that has a definite beginning, middle, and end. The term has been abused by many publishers as the popularity of the format has grown. Many publishers will bind together any superhero story arc and call it a graphic novel. Many stories originally published as individual comics (*Watchmen*, *Bone*, and *Sandman*, for instance) are self-contained series that were intended to tell one single story and not to be an ongoing series, like *Batman* or *Spider-Man*.

Today, graphic novels have told some of the most complex, beautiful, and moving stories in our modern literature. Whether it's Marjane Satrapi's (2004) biographical *Persepolis* or Art Spiegelman's (1996) Pulitzer Prize-winning *Maus: A Survivor's Tale*, graphic novels have transcended their initial perception as "big comic books."

PROJECT

PROFILES IN COMIC CREATION!

Although a variety of creators from all ages of graphic literature are profiled within this book, it comes at the cost of so many other deserving names. For every Stan Lee, there is a Denny O'Neil and for every Jack Kirby, there's a Steve Ditko. Research a writer or artist not already in this book and make a multimedia presentation for class. How did he or she get into the business? What were some of his or her legendary works? What contributions did he or she make to the business that left a lasting mark?

CREATOR:		
MAJOR WORKS:	**WORKED WITH:**	**WORKED FOR:**

PERSONAL DETAILS:

SUPERHEROES

SUPERHEROES VERSUS THE REAL WORLD

Since Superman beat up his first mine owner guilty of abusing his employees, superheroes have grown in maturity. As discussed in the previous chapter, superheroes have helped with the war effort, become disenchanted by government corruption, and dealt with substance abuse problems, both their own and those of the people they love. They may live in a fantastic world filled with superpowers and supervillains, but they have never been able to avoid the realities of the world. For every vulnerability that he or she is forced to overcome to triumph over evil—Superman has kryptonite and the Green Lantern is affected by the color yellow—no amount of X-ray or heat vision, super speed, or super strength can make a superhero immune to society's problems.

Discuss

Do you think that each superhero's vulnerability is symbolic? In what ways?

COMIC BOOKS GROW UP

Discuss

To what do you attribute the shift in tone in graphic literature in the late 1980s? Why do you think creators went in this direction?

By the late 1980s, while comics were still thought of as the province of children, the readers of comics had grown up, and the writers and artists of those comics had grown up, too. Through the end of the 1970s, even the darkest of storylines provided a level of hope that managed to shine through in the end. As the 1970s gave way to the 1980s, that hope was extinguished by a strong level of cynicism that had never previously been present in comics, even through the death of Spider-Man's girlfriend and various characters' substance abuse problems. Always a character who embodied the dark underbelly of society, Batman saw his sidekick Robin be beaten to death in the "Death in the Family" story arc, and Batgirl crippled by a bullet to the spine in *Batman: The Killing Joke* (Moore, 2008), both tragedies courtesy of the Joker. In the late 1980s, Batman was front and center in one of the two seminal works of the decade, Frank Miller's (1997) *The Dark Knight Returns*.

Creator Profile

Frank Miller

Writer and artist Frank Miller was born in Olney, MD, in 1957. Raised in an Irish-Catholic family, and the fifth of seven children to an electrician father and nurse mother, Miller grew up in Montpelier, VT.

He began his comic career as an artist, working on a licensed comic for the classic television series, *The Twilight Zone*, in 1978. He parlayed it into a job at DC Comics, working on two issues of *Weird War Tales*, also in 1978. It was at Marvel that Miller would see his first real success. Making his debut on *Daredevil* in May of 1979, he brought the dark noir style that would come to be his trademark to the comic. He made it a point to make the Hell's Kitchen neighborhood in which Daredevil operated be as authentic as possible, going so far as to sketch the neighborhood's rooftops to capture the look. The move gave the comic a gritty, raw feeling that many comics, even ones set in New York, were void of. Within 2 years, Miller had moved to being the writer and the artist. During his run on the title, he created Elektra, an assassin and love interest for Daredevil.

After leaving *Daredevil*, Miller produced his first creator-owned title with *Ronin* for DC Comics. During this time, Miller pitched a revamp of the company's core characters (Superman, Batman, and Wonder Woman), but it was rejected. Despite this rejection, Miller still got a chance to put his stamp on Batman, as he would write two of the character's definitive stories: *The Dark Knight Returns*, which told the story of the twilight of Batman's career, and *Batman: Year One*, which told of his origins.

By the 1990s, with the exception of a fully painted graphic novel for Marvel Comics that told of the resurrection of Elektra, Miller announced that he intended to release all of his work through up-and-coming publisher Dark Horse Comics. In a decade that saw him dabble in screenwriting, writing the scripts for *Robocop 2* and *Robocop 3*, Miller, through his partnership with the publisher, would have two of his greatest successes since his work on Batman: *Sin City* (2005) and *300* (1999).

Initially serialized in *Dark Horse Presents* #51–#62, *Sin City* would be the culmination of everything that Miller had been doing through various superhero stories over the previous decade. The world of Sin City was one populated by hard-nosed detectives, corrupt cops, virtuous criminals, evil priests, serial killers, and good-hearted bad girls all done in a stark black-and-white art delivered in Miller's trademark style. *Sin City* would be his focus for most of the 1990s. Several of the stories were adapted into a movie by director Robert Rodriguez in 2005.

At the end of the decade, he would have another triumph with *300*, the story of the Battle of Thermopylae. Written and drawn by Miller, with colors by frequent collaborator and then-wife, Lynn Varley, it told of the battle and the events that led up to it through the perspective of the Spartan King Leonidas.

In 2001, Miller and Varley began work on the long-awaited sequel to *The Dark Knight Returns*, *The Dark Knight Strikes Again* (2004). By the time he began work on the title, he had moved from Los Angeles, where he lived for most of the previous decade as he worked on *Sin City*, to New York. However, his original plans for the story would be altered when the September 11th attacks occurred just 4 miles from his home. The story's tone had a noticeable shift as Miller, along with the rest of the world, reacted to the tragedy of that day (the original story included a scene of Batman crashing the Batmobile into a skyscraper).

Today, Miller still lives in New York and works frequently. He has worked on DC's *All-Star Batman and Robin*, which he says is set in the same world as his *Dark Knight* tales. He also directed his first movie in 2008, an adaptation of Will Eisner's iconic *The Spirit*.

- View work by Frank Miller from different genres. What themes do they share? Why do you think he makes these choices?
- View pages from Frank Miller's (2005) *Sin City*, and watch clips of from classic film noir. What do they share in common? Why do you think he chose black and white for the art?

THE DARK KNIGHT RETURNS

In response to the monumental success of Superman, National Allied Publishing requested that more superheroes be created. Artist Bob Kane designed a character initially called "The Bat-Man" and created an early version of the now iconic costume. Along with writer Bill Finger, the Dark Knight was an instant hit after first appearing in *Detective Comics* #27 in May of 1939, and served as a polar opposite of Superman in many ways. Contrary to Superman, who was an alien who came to our planet as the physical ideal of perfection and was raised by loving parents, Bruce Wayne's road to becoming Batman was noticeably darker.

Unlike Clark Kent, who came from a background of love and support that led to his quest to bring peace and justice to a turbulent world, Bruce was shaped by an act of violence as he witnessed his parents' murder during a robbery. Using the considerable resources that he inherited with the death of his wealthy parents, he grew up to wage what was initially a one-man war on crime.

If Superman is the physical ideal of perfection, then Batman represents the mental ideal. A skilled fighter for sure, the Dark Knight's greatest asset is his intelligence. Among his myriad nicknames, the "World's Greatest Detective" is one that he earned through his abilities to deduce. Although other superheroes may have natural physical attributes that exceed his own, Batman's greatest gift has always been his intelligence.

Although the character began life as a loner character who operated in the shadows, the Batman mythos has grown considerably over the years to incorporate an increasingly larger supporting cast. Nearly a year after his debut, Bruce Wayne took in Dick Grayson, an 8-year-old orphan circus performer whose family had died just as tragically as Bruce's, being murdered by a mobster who wanted to send a message to the circus promoter by killing some of the circus performers. Working together to stop the mobster and get justice for the murders, Bruce trained Dick and gave him the title of Robin (the character's appearance was meant to invoke the costume of Robin Hood). Over the years, five different people have held the title of Robin.

Batman's supporting cast also includes Alfred J. Pennyworth, the longtime butler to the Wayne family and the only father figure that Bruce has ever known. His close relationship with Detective James Gordon (later police commissioner) has been one of mutual benefit, as it allows Batman to privately aid the Gotham Police Department while getting inside information in return. In the late 1960s, the daughter of James Gordon, Barbara, joined the Batman family as Batgirl, a title she held until she was crippled by the Joker in *Batman: The Killing Joke* in 1988.

Considered to have one of the largest and most colorful collections of villains, Batman's greatest foe has always been that of the maniacal Joker. Designed as a failed comedian/clown, the Joker's success has come from the fact that he represents the antithesis of Batman. Where the Dark Knight stands for order at all costs, the Joker is a character driven by chaos. Most villains' desire is power and the financial rewards that accompany it, but the Joker has never shown any particular interest in such things. Although his origins have been altered throughout the years, the most recognized is that he began as an engineer who quit his job to become a comedian, only to fail. In the wake of his failure, he was forced by the mob to commit a crime. To show they were serious, they killed Joker's pregnant wife. During the crime, Joker is confronted by Batman and responds by jumping into a chemical vat, an accident which drives him insane and leaves him permanently disfigured with bleached white skin, ruby red lips, and green hair.

One of Batman's greatest foes, however, was perhaps the character's late-1960s television series. The character's darker origins were cleaned to the point of sparkling for the sake of having a character who was wholesome family entertainment. The show presented a campy Batman, and even after the series had long been canceled, writers and artists worked hard to overcome the perception of the character as being silly. Their attempts yielded varying levels of success but mostly failure until 1986, when Frank Miller rebuilt Batman by telling a story at the end of his life that captured the essence of the character.

Even 20 years removed from the Batman television series, the character had unfortunately carried with it the camp that was a trademark of the show. The late 1980s would see the character revitalized by four iconic stories: *The Dark Knight Returns*, *Batman: Year One*, *A Death in the Family*, and *Batman: The Killing Joke*, all of which added a darkness and depth to the character that had been long absent. Readers were treated to the beginning, the middle, the end, and all of the tragedies in between instead of to just the classic cartoon battles that had been rehashed for years. Writer Frank Miller was responsible for two of these tales, *Year One* and *The Dark Knight Returns*.

It was with *The Dark Knight Returns* that the character would be revitalized and made relevant for the first time in years.

Discuss

- How has the character evolved over time? Has he always been a reflection of culture? How is he perceived now?
- Discuss how Batman is representative of the dark side of our culture.
- Frank Miller has done two major works on Batman. Do you believe that they exist in the same world or different?

Themes

The good fight is one of the prevailing themes of both *The Dark Knight Returns* and the Batman mythos in general. Whereas Superman has always stood for hope, Batman has always been a representative of the bleakness of life and the struggle of the everyday battle against evil. Holding true to this theme, the story presents Bruce Wayne 10 years after the last sighting of Batman. He has attempted to retire but a chance encounter with muggers as he returns home from dinner one evening begins to pull him to return to his former secret life.

The specter of death hovers over the story. At the beginning of the story, Bruce has retired from being Batman but is unable to accept a life of being a retiree. Batman is not a character who simply steps away from the life he chose but a character whose final moments must come on his battlefield. At its core, *The Dark Knight Returns* is about being able to die with dignity instead of giving up the fight.

For a character designed to be a loner, Batman has always had a rather large extended family. By the time that *The Dark Knight Returns* is set, Bruce's relationship with Dick (the original Robin) is considerably strained, and Jason Todd (the second Robin) is dead. It was the death of Jason that caused Bruce to vow to never again resume the role of Batman. However, it is in his return to the role that he finds a salvation in Carrie Kelley, who becomes the new Robin. For a person who lost his parents at a young age, Bruce has always been a father figure to an entire generation of lost and lonely children.

Characters

Bruce Wayne/Batman: Now 55, Bruce retired Batman 10 years prior to the novel's beginning. No longer reclusive, he has become an alcoholic. His return as Batman comes with his acceptance that society needs him, despite the personal demons (e.g., guilt and alcoholism) that are otherwise keeping him away.

Alfred Pennyworth: The Wayne family's longtime butler. He has been a private doctor and Bruce's father figure since the death of Thomas Wayne. He is in his 80s now.

Carrie Kelley/Robin: Unlike previous Robins, Dick Grayson and Jason Todd, Carrie is not an orphan but does seem to have neglectful parents. After being saved by Batman, she sets out to meet him and becomes the new Robin. After saving him, she earns his trust and is accepted in the role, making her the first female Robin.

Commissioner James Gordon: A former Gotham Police detective and now commissioner. It is revealed that he has long known of Bruce's double identity and has always been supportive of it. He is 70 at the beginning of the novel, and is on the verge of retirement after serving as commissioner for 26 years.

Ellen Yindel: A Gotham Police Department captain. Ellen is about to succeed Gordon as commissioner. Although she initially is critical of Batman's return, she comes to passively accept him in the wake of the Joker's resurgence.

Harvey Dent/Two-Face: Released after spending the previous 12 years in Arkham Asylum, Dent has received plastic surgery to repair his damaged face (paid for by Bruce Wayne), as well as psychiatric care from Dr. Wolper.

The Joker: Batman's longtime nemesis. The Joker has also been in Arkham Asylum but in a catatonic state. The reemergence of Batman awakens him and returns his psychotic desires, as he plans a crime spree that will lead to his final confrontation with the Dark Knight.

Clark Kent/Superman: Since Batman's retirement, Superman has worked at the behest of the government, which now uses him like a pawn. It is not a position that he enjoys but one he accepts, as it is the only means by which he may still operate since superheroes were federally outlawed.

Oliver Queen/Green Arrow: Always a very liberal character, Oliver has undertaken a campaign against what he sees as government oppression in a world that has since banned superheroes. He lost his left arm following a battle with Superman but continues to fight by using his teeth to draw his bow.

Selina Kyle: Batman's longtime enemy and love interest has given up her double life as Catwoman and now runs an escort business.

Dr. Bartholomew Wolper: A psychiatrist at Arkham Asylum. Wolper declares Batman to be a "fascist" and blames him for Harvey Dent's and Joker's status as criminals, calling them victims of Batman's crusade.

Mutant Leader: The sadistic leader of a mutant gang whose goal is to control Gotham City. He is a physical superior to the much older Batman. Batman is able to defeat him through wit and cunning.

Part 1: The Dark Knight Returns

Why do you think Frank Miller chose to have a girl be Robin, when all previous Robins were boys?

At the beginning of the novel, it has been 10 years since Batman was last seen, and he is now considered to be a myth that never truly existed. Bruce has survived a car wreck, but his body is damaged, forcing him to use a cane. During a dinner with Commissioner Gordon, it is revealed that Gordon has long known of Bruce's secret identity and that a gang of mutants have been sending him death threats.

Following the dinner, Bruce has a chance encounter with muggers, who leave when they realize that he is willing to fight them. Upon his return home, Bruce begins to feel the pull to return as Batman. He shaves off his mustache, the significance of which is only noticed by Alfred.

Harvey Dent, formerly Two-Face, is to be released from Arkham Asylum after receiving plastic surgery to repair his scars and psychiatric care from Dr. Bartholomew Wolper. However, his scarring runs more psychological than it does physical.

Bruce decides to resume being Batman, and the news of this awakens his longtime foe, the Joker.

- Both Commissioner Gordon and Alfred have served as mentors and father figures to Bruce. Do you believe that they have done an adequate job filling in for the deceased Thomas Wayne? Why or Why not?
- Harvey Dent is a character with a dual nature that was long attributed to his disfigurement. What other characters from literature have had the same dual nature? Why do Dent's scars go much deeper than his skin?

ESSENTIAL QUESTIONS

1. At the beginning of the novel, Batman has been retired for 10 years. Was his transformation back to Batman inevitable? Why or why not?

2. Much like the dual nature of good and evil, that one cannot exist without the other, was the Joker's recovery fully possible without Batman's return? Why or why not?

3. Dr. Wolper argues that Harvey Dent and the Joker were victims of Batman's vigilantism. Do you agree that they worsened as a result of their clashes with him? Could such characters ever truly have hope for being rehabilitated?

Part 2: The Dark Knight Triumphant

As Batman wages battle on the mutant gang following an attempt on the life of Commissioner Gordon, someone new is spotted around Gotham dressed as Robin. She eventually earns his trust and acceptance after saving his life during a fight with the mutants.

Joker has begun working on his plan and is attempting to get public sympathy. A former captain in the Gotham P.D., Ellen Yindel, is named as Gordon's successor.

In the second chapter, a new Robin appears, one that Batman comes to accept. If Batman is such a loner character, why does he have such a large extended family?

ESSENTIAL QUESTION

Throughout the history of superheroes, there has always existed an inner turmoil that comes with leading two lives, Batman being a prime example. In *The Dark Knight Returns*, though, we are presented with Carrie Kelley, who seems to have no issues with leading a double life. Why do you feel that she is immune to something that other characters who have held the title of Robin were not?

Part 3: Hunt the Dark Knight

While breaking up a robbery, Batman and Robin are interrupted by Superman. The old friends decide to meet the following day. Following the defeat of their leader by Batman, the mutants have pledged their allegiance to Batman and are fighting crime using lethal means, which he opposes.

The Joker is set to appear to on a late-night talk show. He hatches a sinister plan and escapes the studio and visits former Catwoman, Selina Kyle (now the owner of a call-girl business) and kidnaps one of her clients, a senator. Batman pursues him, setting up their final confrontation.

ESSENTIAL QUESTION

Frank Miller portrays Superman as being something of a sell-out to the government, doing whatever is asked of him without question. Do you believe that Superman has sold out or do you think that he is merely working within the system to accomplish what he otherwise could not?

Part 4: The Dark Knight Falls

Although defeated by Superman, the Soviet Union launches a nuclear warhead at the United States. Superman attempts to stop it. The warhead is designed to send out a large, magnetic pulse. The warhead manages to stop all electronic devices in the country, as well as blot out the sun, which is the source of Superman's power.

Superman has met with the president to discuss how to deal with Batman, who is acting as a vigilante in spite of the new law. Superman acknowledges that the president will not allow him to bring Batman in alive. Meanwhile, Oliver Queen/Green Arrow visits Bruce to discuss the impending confrontation with Superman, which Queen acknowledges as inevitable.

Knowing that Superman will be weakened by the sun not being visible, Batman sets up his confrontation with him in Crime Alley, the place where he saw his parents murdered. He goes into the battle knowing that he will not survive it. He has chosen the location for the symbolic reason that he wants his final moment as Batman to be in the same place where his life as Batman was born.

Throughout their fight, Superman is holding back so as to not kill Batman. Using kryptonite to weaken Superman, Batman is able to keep the fight even for a time. At the end of the fight, Batman falls dead from a heart attack. At the funeral, however, Superman is able to hear Bruce's heart beating and knows that he faked his death. The novel concludes with Bruce meeting with Robin and the Mutants as he lays the groundwork for how they will continue their battle against crime.

ESSENTIAL QUESTIONS

1. Batman comes from a long line of superhero vigilantes, which ranges from the nobility of Superman to the lethality of the Punisher. Are vigilantes, like Batman, good or bad for society? Explain your reasoning and cite at least five examples.

2. Through the comics and recent movies from director Christopher Nolan, Batman has become one of the most popular and enduring superheroes. What do you think is the reason for his appeal? Do people relate to the solitary and disturbed nature of the character or is it something else?

3. Do you feel that graphic novels, such as *The Dark Knight Returns*, are a reflection of our culture? If so, what does that say about it?

Superman and Batman have strongly opposing worldviews. Batman was born of murder, and Superman was born of a selfless act of love. How have their lives come to define their characters?

- Why does Batman so strongly oppose the use of lethal methods to fight crime, particularly guns? What moral distinction is he making? Do you agree or disagree with his stance?
- Superman is referred to by the Green Arrow as a "big blue school boy." Why do you think that Superman's morality is a point of contention for both readers and other characters?
- At the novel's conclusion, Bruce has faked his own death and is planning, along with Robin and the mutants, for something big. Why was it important that the perception be that he has died? What do you believe is his plan?

PROJECT

HEROES REBORN

You are going to meet with the head of a major comic publisher to pitch a project. They're concerned that one of their classic characters has become too stale, and they've asked you to create an updated and edgier version. You're worried because this is an enduring character with a 60-year history, and although you certainly want to do something new and different with the character, you don't want to screw it up and make the fans angry.

THE CAST

The first thing you need to decide is who will be in the comic. You need to choose the hero, the villain, and the supporting cast. Who is your hero and why did you choose him? Who is your villain? Do you choose a marquee villain, such as the Joker or Lex Luthor, or do you choose a lesser known, second-tier villain, such as the Riddler or the Calendar Man? Finally, the supporting cast is very important. Who is Superman without Lois Lane and Jimmy Olsen, or Batman without Alfred or Commissioner Gordon?

The hero:
The villain:
The supporting cast:

THE STORY

This is the most important part. The publisher wants a fresh take on this classic character that will make him edgier. What will you do that is new or different? Obviously, you don't want to write the same "the hero defeats his classic villain" story that readers have seen over and over again. How will you take this character and make it fresh again?

The story:

WATCHMEN

In 1983, DC Comics acquired the rights to the Charlton Comics' characters. Writer Alan Moore (1995) intended to use the characters to develop the story that would become *Watchmen*. However, DC quickly realized that the way Moore intended to use the characters would render them useless in the future, as it left some characters dead and others morally compromised.

Moore was asked to create all new characters for his story. Realizing that many of the Charlton characters were superhero archetypes, he used them as models from which to create his new characters. His plan for the story was to create a real world in which superheroes existed and show them as being more human than they had previously been portrayed. He used the story as a reflection on the anxieties of contemporary culture. Although the story is about the investigation of the murder of a superhero, it portrays the dysfunction of each of the story's protagonists.

Themes

At one point in the novel, "Who watches the Watchmen?" is seen written as graffiti. The idea that absolute power corrupts absolutely is recurring throughout the novel. If superheroes have unlimited power, then what possibilities exist when there is no force to keep them under control? When superheroes like The Comedian become corrupt or Ozymandias begins to see himself as superior to the rest of the world, there is no one powerful enough to stop them.

Despite many of the heroes appearing to be emotionally detached, there are several moments in the novel when the reader sees that behind their masks and powers, the characters are all too human, proving that no one is exempt from emotion. Although he is seemingly emotionless, Doctor Manhattan displays his powerful emotions when he becomes angry or sad. Rorschach's reaction to the destruction of New York displays this same theme.

The dangers of the advancement of technology are exemplified by Doctor Manhattan. After his "rebirth" as Manhattan, Dr. Jon Osterman creates new technology, which inadvertently aids the plan of the story's villain, Adrian Veidt. The advancement of technology, through both Manhattan and Veidt, shows a society becoming neglectful of humanity.

Characters

Edward Blake/The Comedian: Following the government's outlaw of superheroes (a concept mirrored in *The Dark Knight Returns*), Blake is one of only two government-sanctioned superheroes operating, along with Doctor Manhattan. It is his murder that sets the plot into motion. Although he is depicted as being ruthless and nihilistic, he is a character with deep insight into the reality of the effect superheroes actually have, which he views as a joke.

Daniel Dreiberg/Nite Owl: Dreiberg is one of many retired superheroes and now seems to live a boring, empty life. The character has much in common with Batman in that he is a powerless superhero who relies on gadgets and skilled fighting.

Laurie Juspeczk/Silk Spectre: Laurie is the daughter of the first Silk Spectre, Sally Jupiter, and The Comedian. She is girlfriend of Doctor Manhattan.

Walter Kovacs/Rorschach: In spite of the outlaw of superheroes, Rorschach continues to operate as a vigilante. He wears a trench coat, hat, and white mask with a constantly shifting inkblot, which serves as a metaphor for his worldview. He is detached and persistent, but is also paranoid and prone to conspiracy theories.

Dr. Jon Osterman/Doctor Manhattan: One of only two government-sanctioned superheroes, along with The Comedian, Doctor Manhattan was the creation of an accident that occurred when he was trapped inside an Intrinsic Field Subtractor, which gave him power to manipulate time and matter. To avoid being a completely emotionless character, he is infused with human habits, and in fact, his struggle to maintain his humanity is central to the story.

Adrian Veidt/Ozymandias: Veidt is a character whose power comes from his intelligence. He is able to use 100% of his brain power. Veidt's superior intelligence is ultimately his downfall, as he has a god complex and believes that he can save humanity, which makes him the story's villain despite his "good" intentions.

Discuss

In the first chapter, we meet Rorschach, who is quoted as saying that when everyone asks for help, he will say no. Why do you believe that he would be unwilling to help?

Part 1: At Midnight, All the Agents

Police are investigating the murder of Edward Blake/The Comedian, who was thrown from a window. The vigilante Rorschach investigates the murder and discovers that Edward Blake was The Comedian's alter ego. Concerned that someone is targeting members of the superhero group the Watchmen, he seeks out fellow former members Daniel Dreiberg (Nite Owl), Adrian Veidt (Ozymandias), Laurie Juspeczyk (Silk Spectre), and Dr. Jon Osterman (Doctor Manhattan), but none of them seems concerned.

Part 2: Absent Friends

On the day of Blake's funeral, Laurie/Silk Spectre visits her mother, Sally (the first Silk Spectre), who lives in a California retirement home. Sally tells her daughter that she was once sexually assaulted and nearly raped by Blake before another hero stopped him. At the funeral, Doctor Manhattan shares with Daniel and Adrian that Blake killed a Vietnamese woman that he had impregnated while the two were ending the Vietnam War.

ESSENTIAL QUESTION

Despite being portrayed as a rather loathsome human being, Edward Blake's funeral is still attended by many of his friends. Why do you think that they chose to attend when it is clear that many of them did not like him?

At Edward Blake's funeral, Manhattan tells the story of Blake killing a Vietnamese woman in front of him. Why do you believe Manhattan did nothing to stop it?

Part 3: The Judge of All the Earth

Following an argument about Doctor Manhattan's emotional distance, Laurie goes to dinner with Daniel/Nite Owl. After she vents about her relationship problems, the pair is attacked in an alley by a gang, whom they easily dispatch using their superhero fighting skills. During this, Doctor Manhattan appears on a talk show and is ambushed by the host, who accuses him of giving cancer to several former colleagues and one former adversary. An angered Manhattan leaves the planet for Mars.

Part 4: Watchmaker

The chapter covers Doctor Manhattan's backstory. The son of a watchmaker, Doctor Manhattan wanted to follow in his father's footsteps until the United States used the atomic bomb on Hiroshima and Nagasaki, and his father pushed him to instead become a scientist.

He is killed during an accident at the lab but returns, initially as a skeleton but subsequently in a slowly regenerating form as full person with blue skin and superhuman powers. The government recruits him, and he is named Doctor Manhattan, the first "real" superhero.

What signs do we see in Part 3 that Manhattan is becoming more emotionally distant? Do you think that his relationship with Laurie makes this better or worse?

ESSENTIAL QUESTION

Originally intending to become a watchmaker, Jon Osterman constructs a large clockwork mechanism on Mars. How is time used symbolically in the novel?

Part 5: Fearful Symmetry

Learning that Blake had visited a former adversary, Moloch (one of the people who has cancer "due" to Doctor Manhattan), Rorschach, too, visits him to discuss Blake. Realizing that Moloch has nothing to do with Blake's death, he leaves after giving him a place where he may be contacted should he remember anything else.

Adrian Veidt is attacked in an apparent assassination attempt. Although several people are killed, Veidt is able to overpower his attacker but not before the attacker eats a cyanide capsule and kills himself.

Responding to a note received from Moloch, Rorschach returns to visit him, only to find that Moloch has been killed, and that he has been framed for the murder. The police arrive on an anonymous tip about the murder, and although Rorschach initially fights them off, he is taken into custody.

In Part 5, the reader begins to see that there was more to The Comedian than had previously been characterized. Why do you think that a character who is not comical is called "The Comedian"?

Part 6: The Abyss Gazes Also

Now in prison, Rorschach is identified as Walter Kovacs. He meets with a prison psychiatrist who shows him inkblots (called a Rorschach test). All of the cards he is shown invoke disturbing moments from his past that reveal the depths of darkness that exist in Rorschach's mind. One card reminds him of finding a dog with its head split open (he identifies it as a "pretty butterfly"), and another reminds him of being beaten as a child by his mother, a prostitute, after he walks in on her in bed with a man (he identifies the picture as "some nice flowers").

During a follow-up session, he reveals that came to wear the inkblot mask because he realized long ago that humanity is uncaring and selfish and that he needed a face he could stand to look at in the mirror.

As he enters the prison's general population, Rorschach is taunted by numerous inmates that he had helped put in prison. He is attacked by one inmate while getting food in the cafeteria. He disfigures the inmate by throwing hot oil in his face.

During his next session, Rorschach discusses the beginnings of his crime-fighting career. He admits that although he did not like Blake, he respected him because he was the only member of the group with a true understanding of how humanity operated.

In his final therapy session, he admits that one of the inkblot tests reminded him of a dog with its head split open, which reminded him of the night that Walter Kovacs ceased to be. He had been investigating the disappearance of a little girl. When he discovered that the kidnapper had raped and murdered the little girl, Rorschach handcuffed the man to a pipe. Outside the home, the kidnapper's dogs were barking, so Rorschach took out his anger on the dogs by killing them as the kidnapper begged for their lives. Disgusted that the kidnapper would plead for mercy for the dogs but could not show the same mercy to a child, Rorschach left him handcuffed to the radiator and burned down the house. He considered the flames to be a baptism of sorts, and he ceased from that moment forward to be Walter Kovacs, leaving only Rorschach.

Part 7: A Brother to Dragons

No longer with a home after Doctor Manhattan's self-imposed exile to Mars, Laurie is now staying with Daniel. He takes her to his basement hideout and shows her the various Nite Owl gadgets and how they operate. Later that evening, Daniel goes to the basement and laments his inability to fully shed himself of Nite Owl. To help him, Laurie suggests they put on their former costumes and go out in Daniel's ship "Archie," named for Merlin's owl, Archimedes.

While out in the ship, they discover a tenement building that is on fire. The pair is able to save the trapped residents, which reignites their confidence and passion.

Part 8: Old Ghosts

Returning from their night out, Laurie and Daniel discuss whether Doctor Manhattan's exile following the revelations that several former friends have cancer is part of a larger conspiracy to get him off of the planet. Daniel realizes that something is happening and that they must break Rorschach out of prison as soon as possible.

As Laurie and Daniel arrive at the prison to free Rorschach, they discover that a riot has broken out in the prison. Still in his cell, Rorschach is being menaced by a trio of former enemies. After calmly killing all three, he leaves with Laurie and Daniel.

As they arrive at Daniel's hideout, they discover Doctor Manhattan is waiting for them. Laurie leaves with him to Mars, and Daniel and Rorschach leave after the police show up at the house looking for them.

At the news of Rorschach's escape from prison, the same gang that was previously beat up by Daniel and Laurie go looking for Daniel but mistakenly go to the home of Hollis Mason, the original Nite Owl, and beat him to death.

Part 9: The Darkness of Mere Being

On Mars, Manhattan uses his powers to allow Laurie to keep breathing despite the hostile atmosphere, as he takes her to a crystal fortress that he erected.

After his imprisonment, Rorschach is shown a serious of inkblot cards. The images produce disturbing images, but he lies in his responses. Why do you think he lies but later decides to tell the truth?

Why is Daniel unable to let go of being Nite Owl? Do you think that it's out of boredom or that it is a compulsion within him to be a superhero?

Inside, Laurie vents her frustrations that Manhattan's clairvoyance allows him to know all of the details of their conversation before they happen.

They discuss Manhattan's eroding human emotions. He calmly explains that end of the world will also be the end of human suffering, and he therefore has no motivation to stop it.

Manhattan decides to show Laurie the truth about her birth. He places his hand on her head to show her what he can see. Through a series of flashbacks, Laurie comes to realize that Edward Blake, who once attempted to rape her mother, is actually her father. Overcome with anger, Laurie throws a bottle at the walls of the palace, which shatters it around them. After Manhattan erects a force field to protect them, Laurie says that her life is a joke. Manhattan, who has been emotionally detached for most of the conversation, explains that he views her life, born of "chaotic and improbable circumstances" as a "thermodynamic miracle."

Discuss

The overly rational and analytical Manhattan attributes Laurie's life to be a "thermodynamic miracle." Is there room in a scientific mind for the ideas of fate and miracles?

Part 10: Two Riders Were Approaching

As war between the United States and Russia seems more and more inevitable, President Nixon and Vice President Ford are taken to a hideout, and Adrian Veidt leaves for his retreat in Antarctica. He cryptically informs his associates of "a successful delivery." In front of a large wall of televisions, Veidt decides that the war is officially unavoidable.

Not sure whether they are looking for someone who is targeting superheroes or if The Comedian's death is part of a larger conspiracy, Nite Owl and Rorschach set out to investigate and gather information. While at a bar, they meet a hitman who tells them that Veidt's attempted assassination was paid for, but the hitman did not know who took out the contract on him. Before they leave, Nite Owl learns of the murder of Hollis Mason.

The pair leaves to meet with Veidt to get his help and discover evidence that Veidt took out the hit on himself and has left for Antarctica. Before departing for Antarctica to follow him, Rorschach leaves his journal at the offices of a newspaper. Upon their arrival at Veidt's Antarctic retreat, they are immediately discovered by Veidt, who watched the two approaching on his video monitors.

LISTEN

Part 10 is called "Two Riders Were Approaching," a reference to Bob Dylan's (1968) "All Along the Watchtower."

DISCUSS

Discuss the significance of the lyrics as they relate to the chapter.

Part 11: Look on My Works, Ye Mighty

The chapter begins with Nite Owl and Rorschach discussing what Veidt's intentions might be. Meanwhile, Veidt recounts to his friends the story of his life, including the fact that he gave away the vast inheritance he gained following his parents' death to prove that he could succeed completely on his own.

When Nite Owl and Rorschach enter the retreat, they have a brief fight with Veidt, but are easily defeated. Veidt then explains that he realized that Blake was right when he said that their presence would never fully rid the world of evil. He realized that war was becoming inevitable between the United States and Russia because of the proliferation of arms, which caused him to begin formulating plans to stop the war.

Veidt reveals that The Comedian discovered his plot, which was the reason for his murder, and that he staged his own attempted assassination to throw off Rorschach's suspicion. Veidt's plan, which has already been set into motion, was to teleport an alien life form into New York, during which the psychic shockwave killed half of the city's population. By destroying a major city, he planned to draw sympathy for the United States, which would ease tensions between the U.S. and Russia.

ESSENTIAL QUESTIONS

The character of Adrian Veidt takes much of his inspiration from Alexander the Great, as he sees the only path to peace being complete domination. His name, however, comes from a poem by Percy Bysshe Shelley. Read Shelley's (1818/2002) poem "Ozymandias" in class and discuss it using the questions below.

1. What is Shelley saying with this poem and how does the poem define who Adrian Veidt is? Why did he take his name from this poem?

2. Are there political leaders today that you consider to be similar to the Ozymandias of the poem, or is he a different case because he has absolute power? Which leaders would you want to read this poem?

3. What do you think Ozymandias would say if he could see what has happened to his crumbling statue? Would he be humbled or would he find some other way to boast?

Part 12: A Stronger Loving World

Laurie and Manhattan tour the devastation in New York City before teleporting to Veidt's retreat. Although all are horrified by the plot, they agree that if the absurd truth behind the attack on the city were to be revealed, that it had been staged to draw sympathy for the United States, it would send the world back on a course toward self-destruction. Rorschach refuses to abide by the agreement to keep silent because of the lives that were lost in the attack, so Manhattan kills him to ensure his silence.

At the novel's conclusion, Rorschach's journal detailing the events is picked up by a staff member at the newspaper office, who begins to read it.

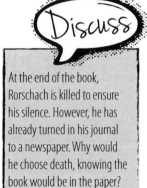

Discuss

At the end of the book, Rorschach is killed to ensure his silence. However, he has already turned in his journal to a newspaper. Why would he choose death, knowing the book would be in the paper?

ESSENTIAL QUESTIONS

1. Throughout the novel, a red-headed vagrant is seen on the streets of New York carrying a sign. It is later revealed that the man is Rorschach without his mask. What evidence tells the reader, prior to the revelation, that it is him?
2. In reviewing the fight between Veidt and his assassin, what evidence exists that the fight was staged?
3. Rorschach, Ozymandias, and Doctor Manhattan are all depicted as being detached from humanity. Why do you think they place a distance between themselves and the rest of the world?
4. What do you think of the way that women are characterized throughout the novel?
5. Doctor Manhattan is the story's one true superhero (he has supreme powers) and is characterized as being emotionally detached. What do you think Alan Moore is saying about god-like omnipotence?
6. What do the back-stories of each superhero reveal about Moore's opinion of humanity?
7. In the wake of New York City's destruction, Adrian believes that he did the right thing and that it all worked in the end. Doctor Manhattan's response is that "nothing ends." What does his response imply?
8. Although it is set in an alternate-reality earth, how does the novel act as a reflection of the times in which it was set?

ESSAY TOPICS

1. Using details revealed throughout the novel, write an obituary for Edward Blake or Walter Kovacs. Be sure to include information about the character's early life, career as a crime fighter, and death.
2. Choose three of the chapter-closing quotations and discuss how each quote ties into the plot of its respective chapter.
3. The novel has several symbolic objects or ideas, such as the smiley face button or time. Explain in an essay why you think these are significant, and support your work with details from the book.

PROJECT

THE NEW WATCHMEN

The genesis of *Watchmen* came about when DC Comics bought the rights to all of the Charlton Comics characters. Moore's pitch left DC realizing that most, if not all, of the characters would be left unusable moving forward, so he instead used the characters as archetypes on which to base new characters.

Taking a cue from *Watchmen*, research a now-defunct Golden Age comic company, such as Ace Comics or Golden Key Comics, and revamp some of the company's characters to tell a modern story. Use the handout to include the characters you chose, how they were originally presented, and how you have revamped them.

Just as Moore did with Watchmen, you must set your comic in the real world:

➤ How would our society react if superheroes were real?
➤ How would they interact with real people?
➤ Where would they live?
➤ What would they do when they weren't fighting crime?

CHARACTER	AS ORIGINALLY DEPICTED	"REVAMPED" VERSION

CHAPTER 3

FANTASY

SUGGESTED TIMELINE 2–3 WEEKS
- Origins/Neil Gaiman profile (1–2 days)
- *Sandman* (1–2 weeks)
  ○ Dream Journal project (1 week)

ORIGIN

The superhero genre of comic books has been one that traditionally contains elements of many genres. In its infancy, there were adventure, detective, humor, war, and western comics. With the advent of the superhero, comic book creators began to blend genres. The first superhero, Superman, was the last son of a dying planet who was sent as a savior to Earth, and many characters who followed him were fantasy-based. In his wake came the mythology-based Wonder Woman and several characters whose powers were attributed to magic in some form, such as The Flash, Green Lantern, and the reincarnated Egyptian prince, Hawkman.

With an increasing interest in science-fiction stories during the late 1950s, the Golden Age of comics gave way to the Silver Age, and many superheroes had their origins reimagined to be more science-based, with The Flash, Green

Discuss

Why do you think that there has been renewed interest in the fantasy genre in recent years?

45

Lantern, and Hawkman all getting revamped origins. However, with the presence of characters such as Marvel's Doctor Strange and DC's Zatanna, a balance was kept between fantasy and science fiction within comics.

Creator Profile

Neil Gaiman

One of the greatest fantasy writers of his generation, Neil Gaiman was born into an Eastern European Jewish family that came to embrace Scientology in the mid-1960s. Gaiman learned to read at the age of 4 and his childhood was filled with J.R.R. Tolkien's *Lord of the Rings* trilogy and the writings of Lewis Carroll, especially *Alice's Adventures in Wonderland*, which had a clear and profound effect on his writing later in life. Amongst the myriad literature he consumed as a child, Gaiman was also a fan of comic books like *Batman* and science fiction.

Beginning his career as a journalist because it was a means by which he could get published and make connections, Gaiman published his first work of fiction in the fantasy magazine *Imagine That* in 1984, when he was 24 years old. That same year, a chance encounter would change his life. As Gaiman waited for a train, he came across an issue of Alan Moore's *Swamp Thing*, which the iconic comics writer had worked on in the early 1980s and revitalized with environmental messages. Gaiman hadn't read a comic book since he was a teenager, but reading Moore's take on the subversive superhero led him to return to a comic shop for the first time in years.

While he continued his journalistic pursuits, it was again Alan Moore that brought Gaiman to comic books. When the two formed a friendship, Gaiman eventually succeeded Moore on the iconic *Marvelman* for Eclipse Comics. After the company went out of business, he went on to write three graphic novels that would pair him with artist Dave McKean. The two would go on to collaborate on several projects over the years, including the extremely successful *Sandman* series and the movie *Mirrormask* for the Jim Henson Company.

It was his work with McKean that landed him at DC Comics, where he wrote the limited series *Black Orchid*. His work on the series garnered him attention from Karen Berger, the future editor of DC Comics' Vertigo imprint. Just as the company let Alan Moore reimagine the Swamp Thing character, Berger hired Gaiman to write a series that would put a new spin on another older character, *Sandman*.

Instead of the gas-mask-wearing superhero that some readers were familiar with, Gaiman imagined the character as an anthropomorphic personification of dreams. The series would run for 8 years from 1989 until 1996 in an incredible 75-issue run. It has been collected into 10 volumes, won numerous awards, and stands as one of the greatest achievements of graphic literature.

Following the conclusion of *Sandman*, Gaiman has mainly focused on novels, although he has made numerous returns to graphic literature. His greatest success as a novelist came with 2001's *American Gods*.

Gaiman has also done work on movies, serving as a screenwriter on films such as *Mirrormask* and *Beowulf*. Many of his graphic novels have been adapted for the screen as well, including *Stardust* and *Coraline*.

Despite his numerous successes with traditional prose novels and Hollywood screenwriting, Gaiman's notoriety will always be firmly be tied to his work in graphic literature. Gaiman himself recognizes this and attributes it to the possibilities of the medium. As a traditional novelist, he has always felt that he was working in a field where many others who came before him produced incredible work. In graphic literature, however, he knew that his predecessors weren't as numerous, which gave him a wider breadth by which to create new, original, and groundbreaking work. While giving a commencement speech called "Make Good Art" (2012a) at Philadelphia's University of Fine Arts after being awarded an Honorary Doctorate of Fine Arts, Gaiman reveled the key to his success as a piece of advice: "But the one thing that you have that nobody else has is *you*. Your voice, your mind, your story, your vision. So write and draw and build and play and dance and live as only you can" (para. 34). A reading of his masterful *Sandman* series will certainly confirm his reasoning.

SANDMAN

A landmark in graphic literature, *Sandman* began in October of 1988 and continued on an impressive run of 75 issues before concluding in March 1996. Its success led to it being one of but a few works of graphic literature to ever appear on *The New York Times* bestseller list, alongside such titles as *Watchmen* and *The Dark Knight Returns* (both presented in Chapter 2).

The concept, a revamp of the 1970s Jack Kirby series, was initially proposed but rejected for Gaiman's DC Comics limited series *Black Orchid*. Gaiman later mentioned it to his future editor Karen Berger, who offered him the opportunity to turn the idea into a series. *Sandman* would go on to not only be Vertigo's flagship title but to also bring in new readers, many of whom did not previously read comics.

The series tells the story of Morpheus, the Lord of Dreams, who is a personified, anthropomorphic interpretation of dreams. The series begins with Morpheus as a prisoner. Upon his escape, he exacts revenge on his captor before he sets out to rebuild his kingdom, which has fallen into disrepair over the course of his 70-year absence. The character would come to embody the qualities of the tragic hero that was first born with Sophocles' Oedipus.

The series alternates locations between Dreaming (Morpheus's home) and our reality, but does venture from time to time to places such as Hell and Asgard. The series included guest appearances from fellow Vertigo stalemates, Swamp Thing and *Hellblazer*'s John Constantine. It also featured occasional cameos from

Morpheus, the protagonist of *Sandman* series, is characterized as an antihero. Read about antiheroes and discuss the qualities of one. Who are some famous antiheroes?

DC superheroes, like Superman, Batman, and the Justice Society, although this was rare.

Themes

The ways in which dreams shape our perception of reality is a recurring theme in *Preludes and Nocturnes* (the first collected volume of the *Sandman* comics, which we'll be focusing on in this chapter) and throughout the entire series. In *Preludes and Nocturnes*, the imprisonment of Morpheus leaves a void in the realm of dreams, which is filled by Dr. Destiny, who has taken one of the totems of power and is using it to control reality. In the comic, as in our real lives, dreams alter the way we perceive our lives, and therefore, our realities.

As embodied by Morpheus's older sister Death, everything has an ending, even for The Endless Family (Morpheus and his siblings). In the story, Morpheus has been imprisoned for 70 years, and upon his return to his realm of the Dreaming, he finds that his kingdom has crumbled in his absence. He soon discovers that not only has his dream world changed but so too has the waking world, Hell, and even himself. It is a story about the importance of recognizing and embracing change as a natural part of life.

Characters

Sandman/Dream/Morpheus: Both the personification and lord of dreams, Dream is a character known by many names (Morpheus, the Sandman, the Dream Shaper, and Oneiros, among them). Like many of the characters in the series, he is an antihero, who, although heroic, is often insensitive, self-absorbed, and relentless in his retributions. He lives in a castle in the ever-changing realm of Dreaming. He is depicted as being a tall, thin man with bone-white skin and raven-black hair.

Roderick Burgess: Born as Morris Burgess Brocklesby and sometimes known as the Daemon King, he is the Lord Magus of an occult organization called the Order of Ancient Mysteries. At the beginning of the story, he has inadvertently kidnapped Morpheus while attempting to kidnap Death. He imprisons him in a glass globe and attempts to reason with him but receives only Morpheus's silence in return. He dies without gaining his desire and leaves the imprisoned Dream to his son, Alex.

Alex Burgess: The son of Roderick. He inherits his father's magical order and continues to keep Morpheus imprisoned. It is implied that his relationship with his father was unhealthy and that he has little interest in pursuing the dreams of his father. When Morpheus escapes, he punishes Alex by making him experience an unending series of nightmares.

Cain and Abel: Based on the Biblical twins, they now live in Dreaming at Morpheus's invitation, doomed to repeat Cain's murder of Abel.

Lucien: The librarian in Dreaming. He informs Morpheus of what has happened while he has been away that has left his kingdom in ruins. He is the keeper of dreams in the Dreaming and is a faithful and trusting servant to Morpheus.

John Constantine: A conman and occult detective, he is characterized as an antihero. When Morpheus escapes his imprisonment and seeks to recover his lost totems of power, Constantine helps him search for one of the three items, a bag of sand, which was purchased by Constantine but stolen by his ex-girlfriend.

Etrigan: A demon in Hell. Etrigan is the son of Belial, the personified form of a demon in many Christian and Jewish texts, and was centuries ago bound by Merlin the Magician to Jason Blood, a member of King Arthur's Court. It is through his bond to Blood that Etrigan remains good, despite being a violent demon. One of Morpheus's totems, a helm, is in the possession of a demon, and on his quest to recover it; Morpheus meets with Etrigan, who takes him to Lucifer.

Lucifer: Based on the English poet John Milton's interpretation of the character in *Paradise Lost*. He is depicted as having grown bored with his role after lording over Hell for 10 billion years. When he is outwitted by Morpheus, he swears vengeance upon him.

John Dee/Doctor Destiny: A criminal scientist, John Dee uses Morpheus's ruby (the last of the totems of power), to create a device that gives powers of Dream to alter reality while Morpheus is still imprisoned by Roderick Burgess.

Death: The second-oldest member of the Endless family (introduced throughout the series as representations of various aspects of dreams. She is the older sister of Morpheus and appears in the last chapter of the story. Unlike previous depictions of Death as a Grim Reaper, she is a perky and nurturing character who understands the value of the lives that she takes. It is in the final chapter that she visits her younger brother to encourage him to break out of his depression and explore the world that he has missed over his seven-decade imprisonment.

Part I: Sleep of the Just

In Wych Cross, England, in 1916, a man named Roderick Burgess attempts to trap Death but instead imprisons Death's younger brother, Morpheus, The Lord of Dreams. Roderick attempts to bargain with Morpheus but receives only silence in return. After 70 years, Roderick dies and leaves the care of the imprisoned Morpheus to his son, Alex, who does not seem to share his father's interests but does desire the power he could gain from controlling the Lord of Dreams.

Morpheus is able to free himself, though, and exacts his revenge on Alex by placing him in a state of perpetual nightmares.

Discuss

Among the characters that live in the Dreaming are the Biblical twins, Cain and Abel. Read the story of Cain and Abel from the Bible (different versions available at http://www.pitt.edu/~dash/cain.html). Why do you believe that Gaiman made them characters of the dream world? What would they possibly represent?

DISCUSS

- Morpheus quotes T.S. Eliot's (1922/2000) poem "The Waste Land" when he says "And I showed him no fear" (p. 50). Read the poem and discuss the inclusion of the line in this chapter and why Neil Gaiman chose to include it.
- Morpheus quotes Puck the Fairy from *A Midsummer Night's Dream* (Shakespeare, 1590/2009) when he says "Lord, what fools these mortals be" (p. 46). Read Act III of the play and discuss the context of the quote in each work.

RESEARCH

Early in the chapter there is a reference to "Aleister and his friends" (p. 14). This is a reference to English occultist Aleister Crowley. Research Crowley and discuss his inclusion in this chapter.

Part 2: Imperfect Hosts

Now free, Morpheus returns to his kingdom in the realm of the Dreaming. Living there are the Biblical twins, Cain and Abel, who are doomed to perpetually reenact Cain's murder of Abel. When the two get into an argument about what to name a gargoyle, Cain becomes angered and kills Abel. After Abel is returned to life, he agrees with Cain and gives the gargoyle the name that his brother suggested, Gregory.

Morpheus meets with Lucien, the keeper of dreams, who explains to him that things have changed considerably over the 70 years that he was imprisoned. Morpheus realizes that in order to rebuild his kingdom of dreams, he must go out to reclaim the three items that comprise his totems of power: a bag of sand, a helm, and a ruby dreamstone.

ESSENTIAL QUESTIONS

1. Now living in the realm of Dream, the Biblical brothers Cain and Abel are doomed to forever relive Cain slewing Abel. This is portrayed in the story as a simple disagreement between siblings over the naming of a pet, which results in the murder. After each death, Abel returns to life, only to repeat the story again. Why do you think the two brothers are doomed to relive the murder over and over again?

2. As the lord of dreams, Morpheus could be interpreted as a metaphor for an author lording over his own works of fiction. This is also hinted at by Lucien, who serves as a librarian of dreams. Do you think that Neil Gaiman intentionally meant for Morpheus to be viewed this way and if so, why?

Part 3: Dream a Little Dream of Me

While Morpheus was imprisoned, conman and occult detective John Constantine purchased the bag of sand. Unfortunately, the bag was stolen by his ex-girlfriend. He agrees to help Morpheus reclaim it. When they find Constantine's ex-girlfriend, they discover that she has been using the sand like a drug, which has permanently destroyed her mind. They realize that the sand was the only thing keeping her alive and that by leaving, she will die painfully. Morpheus takes pity on the girl and gives her a peaceful death to show his appreciation for Constantine's help.

Discuss

Ellie, a little girl who is later trapped in her dream world when Morpheus is imprisoned, is seen earlier in the novel reading *Through the Looking Glass*, the sequel to *Alice in Wonderland*. In this section, she quotes the book when she says "Why, you're the only sort of thing in this dream." Knowing Lewis Carroll's influence on Neil Gaiman, is this a reference only or does the novel directly influence the story?

LISTEN

This chapter includes numerous references to different songs, including "Dream a Little Dream of Me" (Andre, Kahn, & Schwandt, 1968); "Mister Sandman" (Ballard, 1954); "Sweet Dreams (Are Made of This)" (Lennox & Stewart, 1983); "In Dreams" (Orbison, 1963); and "All I Have to Do Is Dream" (Bryant & Bryant, 1958).

DISCUSS

Listen to the songs and discuss the reasons why the author chose to use references to these songs in this chapter.

Part 4: A Hope in Hell

To reclaim his helm, Morpheus must travel to Hell, where it is kept by a demon. At the gates of Hell, he is recognized by the demon Etrigan, who takes him to Lucifer. Lucifer has grown bored with his existence during the 10 billion years he has ruled Hell. He places Morpheus in a battle of wits against the demon who has the helm. When Morpheus defeats the demon and reclaims the helm, Lucifer becomes angry and swears vengeance on Morpheus.

Part 5: Passengers

Doctor Destiny, who has been in Arkham Asylum, escapes and takes a woman hostage, forcing her to drive him in his quest to reclaim Morpheus's ruby that was once in his possession. He has been in possession of Morpheus's ruby, the last item of the totems of power.

Morpheus seeks the help of the Martian Manhunter, the last surviving Martian and a member of the Justice League, who tells him that his ruby is being stored in a warehouse. Although he is able to find the ruby, it is taken from him by Doctor Destiny, who leaves Morpheus unconscious on the floor of the warehouse.

ESSENTIAL QUESTION

In what was a genre-jumping storyline that incorporated many different characters and elements from the DC Comics universe, Morpheus meets the Martian Manhunter. We see Morpheus as a tall, thin man with bone-white skin, dark clothes, and raven-black hair. However, when Martian Manhunter meets him, his appearance changes. Why do you think this would happen upon meeting something that is not human?

Part 6: 24 Hours

At a diner, Doctor Destiny uses the ruby to alter the realities for everyone inside the diner and forces them to live out various nightmares. After Doctor Destiny tortures the diner patrons over several hours, Morpheus arrives to find everyone dead and Destiny waiting for him. Destiny doubts that Morpheus is powerful enough to defeat him.

MULTIMEDIA

Read portions of John Milton's (1667/2005) descriptions of Lucifer in *Paradise Lost* and view other depictions of him in other media (films, music, and other literature) and compare them to the way he is depicted in this chapter.

DISCUSS

- Lucifer is depicted as having become bored with his role as the Lord of Hell. Why do you think the author characterized him this way?
- Morpheus refers to "the Wood of Suicides" (p. 108), which was in Dante Alighieri's (1308/2013) *Divine Comedy*. Read the excerpts that deal with the Wood of Suicides from "The Inferno" (p. 118–124) and compare and contrast the depiction of Hell in this section with that in Dante's vision.

When Morpheus appears to the Martian Manhunter, he appears in an alien form. Why would his appearance change based on who he appears to?

READ

Part 7's title is taken from Shakespeare's (1603/1998) *Macbeth*. Read Act V, Scene V

DISCUSS

Discuss the connections between it and this chapter.

RESEARCH

John Dee's (Doctor Destiny) dream includes elements of *Julius Caesar* (Shakespeare, 1599/1991), *Macbeth* (Shakespeare, 1603/1998), and *Oedipus Rex* (Sophocles, 429 BCE/1991). Research these plays.

DISCUSS

How do they relate to the dream and why did the author choose them?

Part 7: Sound and Fury

As they battle, Doctor Destiny makes it clear that his intention is to use the ruby to kill Morpheus. Believing that it will kill him, Destiny smashes the ruby. However, it only serves to restore Morpheus's power.

Realizing that the ruby, which is not meant for humans, had destroyed part of Destiny's mind, Morpheus decides not to punish him. He returns him to Arkham Asylum and puts him into a deep, restful sleep without dreaming.

Part 8: The Sound of Her Wings

In the story's epilogue, Morpheus is visited by his older sister, Death. Although Death has long been presented in Western culture as a dark and gloomy Grim Reaper, Death is a pretty girl who dresses all in black. Seeing that her brother is depressed and withdrawn, she encourages him to reacquaint himself with the world that he has been missing for the last 70 years.

Death invites him to leave with her while she returns to work, and they discuss life. After they depart at the end of the day, Morpheus realizes that he must rebuild his kingdom and feels revitalized by the day with his sister and the work that lies ahead.

ESSENTIAL QUESTIONS

1. In the story, Morpheus must regain his power by recovering the three totems of power in order to restore his realm. What symbolism does each of the items hold, and how are they significant to him?
2. Literature is filled with great antiheroes, such as Oedipus Rex, Jay Gatsby, and Winston Smith. In what ways is Morpheus an antihero?
3. In the story's conclusion, Morpheus meets with his older sister, Death. Why do you think that Gaiman decided to portray her in the manner that he did and what does it say about the author's view of death?

PROJECT

DREAM JOURNAL

The Sandman is set in the world of dreams. Even when the character crosses over into the real world, it is in an almost dream-like state. The world of dreams is filled with metaphors for life and allusions to different aspects of our culture.

Over the course of a week, keep a notebook and pen by your bed and record your dreams first thing in the morning in as much detail as possible. Take the journal entries and rewrite them, clarifying the details. Give each dream a title, like the chapter in a book or the subtitle or a movie. After each entry, write a reflection on the dream. What recurring themes did you notice? Using the entire week of dreams, write a story using the recurring themes and motifs in the dreams.

_____

_____

_____

_____

_____

_____

_____

_____

_____

_____

_____

_____

_____

_____

_____

_____

CHAPTER 4

SCIENCE FICTION

HISTORY OF SCI-FI COMICS

The popularity of science fiction in all media was born, in part, out of fear. The dropping of the atomic bomb ended World War II but led to fear of nuclear war during the Cold War with the Soviets. The U.S. Senate held meetings on un-American activities during the "Red Scare" of communist paranoia. The Senate also held hearings about the dangers of comic books in promoting juvenile delinquency. The fear of the 1950s could be summed up as the fear of "the other"—that nameless, faceless threat that existed in the darkness of our hearts and minds, whether the fears were justified or not.

Science fiction has long reflected the fears of society. Similarly, many science fiction films of the 1950s commented on the prevailing fears in society, with

**SUGGESTED TIMELINE
3–4 WEEKS**
- History/Alan Moore profile/ Guy Fawkes prereading/ Plato prereading (1 week)
- *V for Vendetta* (2–3 weeks)
  ○ Back to the Future project (2–3 days)

MULTIMEDIA
Read about the Cold War and view clips from 1950s science fiction films.

DISCUSS
How do the films serve as a metaphor for the paranoia of the time?

many aliens being metaphors for invading Soviets, such as in *The Thing From Another World* (Hawks & Nyby, 1951).

Science fiction in comic books reached its pinnacle of popularity during this time. E.C. Comics published science fiction comics of increasing sophistication, but the company was almost driven out of business with the publication of Dr. Fredric Wertham's (1954) book, *Seduction of the Innocent*, and the subsequent Senate hearings. The company returned in the late 1960s, and they did so publishing alternative, counter-culture comics. The early 1980s introduced a new wave of comics out of Britain that had a focus on fantasy, horror, and science fiction. Writer Alan Moore spearheaded this movement.

Creator Profile

Alan Moore

A magician and occultist like his character John Constantine, British writer Alan Moore is a looming presence over graphic literature. He has been a trailblazer in nearly every genre he has worked in, creating such landmark works like *Watchmen* (1995), *V for Vendetta* (2008), *From Hell* (2000), and *The League of Extraordinary Gentlemen* (2002).

Born in Northampton, Northamptonshire, England in 1953, Moore grew up in a neighborhood that was marked by a high level of poverty and a low level of literacy. Nevertheless, Moore enjoyed the neighborhood that first fostered his love of comic books. One of the most advanced students at his school, Moore qualified for grammar school and immediately experienced culture shock when he arrived at a school populated by middle-class students. After going from being one of the top students at his old school to one of the lowest at grammar school, Moore quickly came to dislike school and lost all interest in academic study.

By the 1960s, he started publishing poetry and prose in his own fanzine, called *Embryo*. By the 1970s, Moore bounced from odd job to odd job but could not find any work that was fulfilling to him. He quit his office job and began writing and illustrating his own comic strip. After having a *Judge Dredd* script rejected by publisher 2000AD, Moore found work with the publisher writing for its anthology series, *Future Shocks*. The work landed Moore jobs at Marvel UK and Warrior, where he began writing *V for Vendetta* in 1982. Also in that year, Moore started writing *Marvelman* (later *Miracleman*), which was a contemporary take on a superhero set in the real world (a recurring theme in his work). Warrior went out of business before either series ended but each was resurrected and concluded later at different publishers.

In 1983, Moore was given the opportunity to resurrect an undervalued DC Comics character, Swamp Thing. After taking over the strip, Moore completely revamped the character's back story, which placed him as part of a long line of monsters, and the stories became environmentally based.

His success on the series led to Moore's seminal work, *Watchmen*. *Watchmen* was first published in 1985, and the 12-part story was wildly successful for the publisher, which led to more work for the company. He would also write the "final" Superman story, *Whatever Happened to the Man of Tomorrow?*, and *Batman: The Killing Joke* (2008a), which saw the psychotic clown character Joker crippling Batgirl by shooting her in the spine.

After reaching the heights of his craft during his tenure with DC, Moore left the publisher following the final issue of *V for Vendetta* and vowed to never return because he was denied royalties on many of the titles that he worked on or created, including *Watchmen*. After a few years of working on independent comics, he made a return to major publishers, working with Image Comics, an upstart company founded on the idea of creator rights and creator-owned titles. When Jim Lee, one of Image's publishers, offered Moore his own imprint, he responded by founding America's Best Comics. As he made plans for titles and hiring publishers, Moore found himself working for the company that he once vowed to never work for again, selling his Wildstorm Productions, including America's Best Comics, to DC Comics.

Under America's Best Comics, Moore produced several works that stand along with his best, including *The League of Extraordinary Gentlemen*, *Tom Strong*, *Top Ten*, and *Promethea*. After nearly 10 years, Moore left his partnership with DC Comics and has since continued his work, including new *The League of Extraordinary Gentlemen* titles, for independent publishers.

In 2010, Moore appeared as himself in an episode of *The Simpsons* (Selman & Kruse, 2007) in which Bart meets Moore at a comic book convention. In the episode, Moore delivers a diatribe about his very real feelings about his books being turned into films. Moore has long opposed being involved or even compensated for the film adaptations of comics. *From Hell*, *The League of Extraordinary Gentlemen*, *V for Vendetta*, and *Watchmen* have all been made into films, with Moore refusing to have his name involved in any way and turning down any royalties.

V FOR VENDETTA

In 1975, a 22-year-old Alan Moore submitted a script for a comic that was rejected because the editor considered the main character to be a transsexual. Years later, when Warrior Comics asked artist David Lloyd to create a new character that was a masked avenger, Lloyd recruited Alan Moore, who revived his original pitch and modified it to create the character of V.

When the British political climate changed in 1983, Moore worried that it left the door open for fascist control in England. His fears were put into the Britain of *V for Vendetta*, which was a dystopian story in the vein of George Orwell.

RESEARCH AND DISCUSS

Moore was inspired by political change in the early 1980s. Research and discuss what happened that might have inspired him.

Prereading: Plato's Allegory of the Cave

Born into a wealthy family, Plato was destined for a political career until the death of Socrates altered the course of his life and led him to become a philosopher. He opened a school that was dedicated to Socrates's vision. The school lasted through the remainder of his life and for many years after.

Plato's writings were in the form of a dialogue between characters. In "The Simile of the Cave" from his work *The Republic* (380 BCE/2007, pp. 240–249), he symbolically discusses the problem that humanity finds itself in and proposes how they might find a solution. Thematically, it shares much in common with Moore's ideas in *V for Vendetta*. Much like the relationship between V and Evey, Plato believes that a teacher cannot teach a student but that the student must have his or her mind directed toward the important things in life, which he does by allowing the student to find the answers on his or her own.

Read the "The Allegory of the Cave" from Plato's *The Republic* and discuss how they relate to the same ideas that Moore puts forth in *V for Vendetta*.

Guy Fawkes and the Gun Powder Treason

In 1604, a group of English Catholics decided to strike back against the oppression by the Protestant King James. The group of 13 conspirators plotted to blow up the House of Lords during the State Opening of Parliament, which would have killed several other key figures.

The conspirators had set up 36 barrels of gun powder under the House of Lords. When an anonymous letter was received by Lord Monteagle, who shared it with King James, a search was ordered. On November 5, 1605, Fawkes was found at his position with the barrels of gun powder. Fawkes was tried, along with seven of the conspirators, and was found guilty. He was executed on January 31, 1606.

In the wake of his execution, the British would celebrate "Guy Fawkes Night" and burn an effigy Fawkes in recognition of King James surviving the attempt on his life. Despite his infamy, Fawkes has since come to be toasted as "the last man to enter Parliament with honest intentions."

RESEARCH

Research the Gunpowder Plot. Guy Fawkes and the conspirators were going to murder King James and several members of Parliament.

DISCUSS

What nonlethal methods could they have used to bring about change?

Themes

V for Vendetta is a speculative fiction novel that shows a London of the future that is run by a totalitarian government. It follows in a literary tradition of George Orwell's (1949/1983) *1984* and Aldous Huxley's (1932/2006) *Brave New World* in that it presents a "future" dystopian society. The Norsefire Party, much like the Nazi Party, controls its citizens through force and fear tactics and has imprisoned and killed its citizens for not conforming to society's norms. As such, a fascist government seeks to exert complete control over all aspects of society.

The character V believes that the people should rule and that government should be abolished, and that doing so embodies all of the principles of anarchy. His extreme views come as a result of the brutality of the Norsefire Party. He wishes for the citizens of London to be able to govern themselves.

Although he is the central figure of the novel, V himself is an enigma. The reader never fully learns his back story, and his characterization is presented mostly from the viewpoints of others, such as Evey and Eric Finch. He is a terrorist, but his terrorist acts are morally ambiguous because they are presented as heroic, despite the destruction that they cause. The character's lack of a true identity allows the reader to judge him solely on his words and actions.

Characters

V: The lone survivor of an accident at a government concentration camp that left everyone dead but imbued him with superhuman powers. He wears a Guy Fawkes mask and the reader never sees his actual face nor learns his true identity or back story. He operates as an anarchic terrorist.

Evey Hammond: A teenager working in a factory whose family has all been killed by the Norsefire Party. She is saved from the Fingermen (the Norsefire Party's secret police) by V. The two form a strong bond, and she eventually succeeds him and carries on his cause.

Adam Susan/"The Leader": The leader of the Norsefire Party. He believes that civil liberties are a dangerous thing. He a solipsistic character who is in love with the computer system called Fate.

Eric Finch: The chief of the New Scotland Yard and Minister of Investigations. Finch is a character who does not agree with the actions of the government but reluctantly follows along, managing to remain a morally strong character.

Lewis Prothero: The former commander of Larkhill, the concentration camp that both housed and created V. Prothero became the Voice of Fate upon leaving the camp. In his charge as the Voice of Fate, he broadcasts "information" to the citizens of London.

Derek Almond: A high-ranking official in the Norsefire Party who runs the secret police force.

Rosemary Almond: The abused wife of Derek. Her life spirals out of control and into a world of desperation after her husband is killed by V.

Dominic: The protégé and partner to Inspector Finch. It is Dominic who first makes the connection between V and the Larkhill staff.

READ AND DISCUSS

Look at excerpts from *1984* (pp. 3–18) and *Brave New World* (pp. 4–20) and discuss dystopias.

RESEARCH AND DISCUSS

V is an anarchic character, who distrusts governments. Research anarchist groups and discuss the source of their distrust.

DISCUSS

Moore chose to not reveal many details about V's back story. Why do you think he chose to keep the character so secretive?

RESEARCH

Adam Susan, "The Leader," believes that only he and Fate are real. Research the concept of solipsism.

DISCUSS

Discuss those who believe in it.

BOOK 1: EUROPE AFTER THE REIGN

Chapter 1: The Villain

Young Evey prepares to go out for the night. When she is caught on the street by the Fingerman, the Norsefire Party's secret police, they plan to rape and murder her. Before they are able to exact their intentions, they are attacked by a man in a black clothes and a Guy Fawkes mask. He quotes Macbeth before dispatching both men with knives.

The two escape to a rooftop, where V reveals to Evey that he is out to celebrate the 5th of November. After reciting a poem about Guy Fawkes and the Gunpowder Plot, he blows up the Old Bailey Courthouse.

Chapter 2: The Voice

V takes Evey to his home to protect her. The home, which he calls the "Shadow Gallery," is filled with forbidden artwork and literature that has been banned by the government.

Meanwhile, television personality Lewis Prothero acts as the "Voice of Fate" and is a personification of the decisions of Fate. Fate is a computerized organization that controls all aspects of a citizen's life. Prothero is aboard a train, telling stories to his friends when the train is boarded by V, who attacks the men and kidnaps Prothero.

Chapter 3: Victims

Eric Finch, the Minister of Investigation, comes to the crime scene on the train, where he finds several mutilated bodies, a "V" mark on the wall, and a single Carson rose. Finch meets with the Leader about the terrorist that they are calling "Code Name V" because of the "V" marks they are finding at the scenes of his crimes. They both express concern over the missing Prothero because a change in the voice of Fate may cause unrest among the citizens.

Chapter 4: Vaudeville

Prothero is being held at the Shadow Gallery as a captive by V, who takes him on a tour of his recreation of the Larkhill Resettlement Camp, a concentration camp. Prothero denies having anything to do with the camp, unaware that V was a prisoner at the camp while Prothero was a guard. On the stage, V has a

RESEARCH AND DISCUSS

Evey is harassed and attacked by the Fingermen. Research the Nazi Gestapo and discuss their control tactics.

DISCUSS

V seems to have a complicated relationship with justice. He seems to care for it deeply while being angered by how it is being carried out. Discuss his conflicted feelings.

The Shadow Gallery is full of banned items. Why would the government ban art in all its forms?

From his symbol, to the repetition of V-words, to the Roman numeral V, the letter V has significance in this story. Why do you think the author chose it?

door marked with the Roman numeral V—the room in which V himself was held prisoner.

Chapter 5: Versions

Norsefire Party leader, Adam Susan, makes his first appearance as he explains in discussion with party members how fascism came to England. Susan is aware of the fact that he is not loved in England but does not care because his true love is Fate, who tells him what the people need to know every day. Meanwhile, V visits the Justice statue on top of the Old Bailey Courthouse and lets her know that she has lost her way.

Chapter 6: The Vision

As all of the party officials are going to Sunday mass, Derek Almond, a high-ranking member of the Norsefire Party, admits that the government covered up the destruction of the Old Bailey Courthouse as being a "planned demolition." He then yells at his wife, who has done nothing to help him vent his frustrations.

It is also revealed by Bishop Lilliman, who also once worked at Larkhill, that Fate dictates the content of the sermons every week. He also admits to his weaknesses, which include young girls. A young girl is brought to his room, and it's Evey.

Chapter 7: Virtue Victorious

Left with the Bishop, Evey attempts to stave off his advances. She convinces him to read from his sermons for her. As he does so, she opens a window to "let in some air," but it is actually to allow V to enter. As he attempts to rape Evey, V enters and kills him.

Chapter 8: The Valley

When Dominic and Finch arrive at the Bishop's to investigate, they find him and his guard dead. There was a recorder running in the room, and it is revealed that V was a prisoner at Larkhill. Evey is now considered to be an accomplice.

Chapter 9: Violence

Upon returning to Shadow Gallery, Evey is upset that V included her in a murder. She eventually apologizes and accepts her role in the killing but indicates that she is against murder. She realizes that despite her desire to help him, she does not know V's full plan.

Dominic and Finch are studying the case and realize both the Bishop and Prothero are linked to Larkhill. They connect this fact to their disappearance.

Chapter 10: Venom

Dominic and Finch start looking into anyone who was involved with Larkhill and discover that every person they find is now dead. All of the deaths appear to be of natural causes, but they are quick to suspect that V is behind each one.

Chapter 11: The Vortex

On Christmas Eve, Finch is giving his report to Mr. Susan, which includes that V had killed Dr. Surridge, a doctor at the concentration camp, by injecting her with poison. When Derek shows up to warn the last person named on the list, a woman named Delia, he discovers that he is too late. He faces V and is quickly killed.

Finch has the doctor's diary, which he shares with Susan. The diary details not who V is, but what he is, an inmate who was given hormone experiments.

BOOK 2: THIS VICIOUS CABARET

Prelude

Book 2 begins with a song that V performs, which describes the ways the government has become corrupted. He concludes the song by singing that the government needs to adhere to its people and not the other way around.

Chapter 1: The Vanishing

Still living with Evey now that she is a suspect, V entertains her with a magic trick. After staying with V for awhile, Evey is confused as to why he has not made any romantic advances. She wants to know if V is her father or has children. He only tells her that he is not her father.

Chapter 2: The Veil

Following the death of her husband, Rosemary Almond is left to ponder the future. The government immediately cuts her off and leaves her with no source of income, despite Derek having given his life in its service. She agrees to go to dinner with Roger, a man who worked with her husband, knowing that his intentions are not pure.

As both Rosemary and Evey try to find ways to survive in the world, V wanders through the streets and ponders on how all of us, every day, are just trying to survive.

Chapter 3: Video

V sneaks into a television studio with explosives strapped to his body. He takes command of the broadcast and delivers a cryptic message that London has not been living up to its potential and that he is going to have to let it go.

Chapter 4: A Vocational Viewpoint

As his broadcast continues, V commends the people for the accomplishments they have made, such as landing a man on the moon. He condemns them, however, for electing to power the people who ruined the government. At the conclusion of his broadcast, V fights his way out of the studio.

Chapter 5: The Vacation

After Dr. Surridge's death, Finch is relieved of his duty and sent on a vacation. Peter Creedy, who replaced Derek, cannot figure out how V knew enough about Jordan Tower to be able to so easily infiltrate the building. It is revealed that in the raid of the building, security discovered Roger Dascombe, who was forced to wear V's costume. They shot him believing him to be V.

Evey has taken residence with an older man named Gordon. Rosemary has been forced to work in a cabaret show to make money.

Chapter 6: Variety

While Evey is on a date with Gordon at the cabaret club, she spots Rosemary sitting alone at another table. She does not know her but recognizes her from the news. When Rosemary is approached by a man at the club who tells her that she has no credit and must leave, Evey, oblivious to the details of the conversation, is happy to see someone talking to Rosemary.

Evey feels abandoned by V but does not realize that he is keeping track of her and watching her every move.

Chapter 7: Visitors

Gordon and Evey have begun a romantic relationship. Two months later, Gordon has visitors one evening. He tells Evey to lock herself in the bathroom until after they leave. Gordon refuses to let the men, organized crime boss Alistair Harper and his henchman, into the house. They argue through the door. Gordon had been involved in a bootlegging business with Harper. Harper's henchman slices through the door with a sword and kills Gordon.

When Evey leaves the bathroom hoping it is finally safe, she sees Gordon lying dead and has flashbacks of her family being killed.

Chapter 8: Vengeance

Evey wanders out into the streets alone. As she walks along, she encounters Rosemary, who is searching for the door into the cabaret club. Evey is unable to help her and hides in an alley with a gun, awaiting Harper, who is supposed to have a meeting with Creedy. As he nears, Evey prepares to kill him but is knocked unconscious before she can shoot him.

Chapter 9: Vicissitude

Evey has in which she is dressed in the same dress she wore to meet the Bishop. In her dream, she encounters Gordon and her mother. When she wakes up, she is alone in a prison cell.

Chapter 10: Vermin

Evey is kept alone in her cell and given her meals through a slot in the door. When the sun sets, she is alone in the dark. Eventually, her captors blindfold her and take her to an interrogation room where she is shown a video from the year before of her on the streets working as a prostitute. When V appears on screen, she realizes that they know that she is his associate.

Evey is once again blindfolded and taken to another room where her head is shaved. She is then returned to her cell. As she cries on the floor, she discovers a five-page letter written on toilet paper by a woman named Valerie who was imprisoned in the same cell.

Chapter 11: Valerie

Evey continues to read Valerie's letter. In it, she details her life from childhood and her struggles with finding acceptance from her family about her sexuality. Evey reads the letter in between bouts of being tortured by having her head dunked in water and being interrogated about V. She refuses to give any details about him. Valerie's story becomes a sanctuary to Evey.

READ AND DISCUSS

Valerie's narrative seems to share much in common with Anne Frank's (1947/1993) *The Diary of a Young Girl*. Read excerpts from the book and compare them to Valerie's letter.

ESSENTIAL QUESTIONS

What is it in Valerie's story that is so inspiring to Evey? How did the story inspire V?

Chapter 12: The Verdict

A guard comes to Evey and attempts to strike a bargain with her. If she gives up V, she will receive a reduced sentence and be given a job working for the secret police. She again refuses, and the guard leaves her alone in her cell with the door open. As she ventures out into the corridor, she discovers that the guards are all mannequins. She discovers the interrogation room only to find another mannequin is the interrogator. There is a tape recorder that has a voice reading the questions she was asked.

After leaving the interrogation room, she continues down the corridor before finally walking through a door and finding herself in V's home, the Shadow Gallery.

Chapter 13: Values

Upon her discovery that V was behind her imprisonment, torture, and interrogation, Evey reacts with anger. V explains to her that he had to do it because he loves her and wanted her to be free from the mental prison that society placed her in and that she has been in her whole life. She goes through the stages of acceptance before V takes her outside. She stands in the rain and accepts everything as the water pours over her.

Chapter 14: Vignettes

Some time has passed, and Evey looks healthy and has regrown some of her hair. She approaches V, who is playing piano, and kisses his mask and thanks him. She believes that Valerie's letter was a part of the hoax of her imprisonment, and V proves to her that Valerie was a real person who was next to him in room Number 4 at Larkhill.

BOOK 3: THE LAND OF DO-AS-YOU PLEASE

Prologue

It is the 5th of November once more. At the Ear, a government area that records the audio of everything citizens say in public and private, Dominic and Mr. Etheridge are working late. Etheridge asks about V, but Dominic says that there has been no new information in almost a year.

Back at the Shadow Gallery, Evey is clearing her room of all things that remind her of her childhood. Evey asks V if he's planning something. He tells her that the end is near.

V gets on top of a skyscraper, conducting a mock symphony as he blows up two buildings, one of which is Jordan Tower. He takes pleasure in the destruction, as if it were a work of art. The Voice of Fate goes on the air and tells everyone that for a 3-day period, they will not be monitored in any way.

Chapter 1: Vox Populi

All over London, the citizens are torn about their new freedom, not sure whether it is a hoax or not. One girl tests the cameras to see if they're on or not. She curses at the camera before producing a can of spray paint, which she uses to paint V's trademark on a brick wall.

Although the reports are that the people are behaving themselves, the government decides to not take any chances and sends out reinforcements.

Chapter 2: Verwirrung

The Leader appears to be losing his mind as he sits and watches all of the chaos in the streets on several video monitors, not interacting with anyone.

Rosemary purchases a gun in the back alley behind the gun shop. She claims that she needs the gun to defend herself, which the gun shop owner does not believe.

Harper is cornered by Creedy and accused of taking part in shady dealings, which he denies. Creedy blackmails him into helping his cause.

Chapter 3: Various Valentines

Harper is now accepting bribes in exchange for "police protection." He accepts a meeting in private with Helen Heyer, the scheming wife of Conrad Heyer, who controls The Eye. She wants Harper's protection to ensure that Conrad will be alive to become the new leader so that she may take advantage of his position to increase her own power.

Rosemary performs at the cabaret club and reflects on the events that have led her to dancing for money. Her life is completely different now.

Dominic is reading the "love letters" that were confiscated that morning during a round-up. He questions the sanity of the people who have been writing the letters, as he sees it as a sign of the further deterioration of society. After considering the letters, he comes to a sudden realization and quickly leaves the office.

Chapter 4: Vestiges

In an attempt to understand V's perspective in order to get in his head and crack the case, Finch visits Larkhill and takes LSD. While he walks around waiting for the drug to take effect, he meets several dozen people who seem pleased to see him and notices he is wearing an inmate's uniform. He sees minorities and homosexuals being taken away.

Discuss

Finch's use of drugs to understand V causes severe hallucinations. Describe his hallucinations and determine what significance each vision holds to the narrative.

Chapter 5: The Valediction

Evey approaches V at the Shadow Gallery to ascertain what his next move will be. She sees that among all of the chaos, V is doing nothing. V walks Evey through the corridors and explains to her that all of his efforts were to pass knowledge on to her. They arrive at a room with a computer that is linked the government's source for everything, Fate.

In yet another room, there is a large bank of video monitors, like the Leader's room. He then takes her to his rose garden and finally to a train filled with flowers.

Chapter 6: Vectors

During a meeting with Conrad, Helen talks about Susan making a public appearance to calm the people. She's intrigued as to why Creedy believes that he will be a more effective leader.

Alone with Fate, Susan seems upset about something. After he is briefly interrupted by an officer, he leans forward and apologizes to Fate and kisses it.

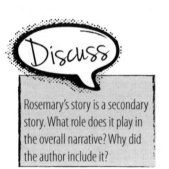

Discuss

Rosemary's story is a secondary story. What role does it play in the overall narrative? Why did the author include it?

Chapter 7: Vindication

During his public appearance, Susan is approached by Rosemary, who shoots and kills him. Meanwhile, Mr. Finch runs into V in an abandoned subway tunnel. Startled by his presence, Finch shoots at V several times. V explains that he cannot be killed because ideas are bulletproof. V stabs him in the shoulder and leaves. After V leaves, Finch finds a trail of blood and believes that he has killed him and returns to Scotland Yard to report the death.

Chapter 8: Vultures

Rosemary has been immediately taken into custody after killing Mr. Susan and is being interrogated. They accuse her of working in conjunction with V. It is revealed that Finch will temporarily replace him as the leader. It's at this moment that Finch comes in to announce that he has killed V. Dominic questions Finch about killing V, and Finch claims to not remember the details very well.

Creedy announces to the people that the terrorist "Code Name V" is dead and that he insurrection has ended.

Chapter 9: The Vigil

V is indeed mortally wounded as he returns home. Evey waits with him as he dies. She removes his mask and imagines that he looks like Gordon and then her father. She thinks about how many people she has lost in her life. In his final moments, Evey finally realizes that V hasn't just been training her to replace him someday, but imminently, as he had anticipated his own death.

Chapter 10: The Volcano

People are gathering in the streets after seeing V's symbol. Although they are not his staunch followers, they have come to respond to his symbol. Dominic realizes that people don't respond to people but to symbols.

While the people are gathered in the street, they are addressed by "V," which is actually Evey wearing his clothes, who announces that his death has been exaggerated.

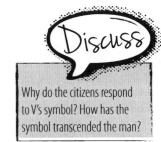

Why do the citizens respond to V's symbol? How has the symbol transcended the man?

Chapter 11: Valhalla

It is now November 10th and Evey prepares to give V a Viking funeral in a train car loaded with explosives, which was his request. In his death, Evey vows to end the killing that V felt was necessary and to provide guidance to the people as they rebuild society. She sends off the car and goes to the roof to see the explosions when the car arrives at 10 Downing Street, the Prime Minister's office.

Dressed as V, Evey brings Dominic to the Shadow Gallery, where it is presumed that he will now be trained, just as Evey once was.

In the street, Helen sees Finch walking and runs to him for help after the mob turns over her car. When he refuses her, she begins berating him with homophobic slurs that he ignores.

Discuss

- With V's death, Evey vows to carry on his work but to do so nonviolently. Do you think she can be as effective without violence? Can she even be more effective? How?
- Why did Evey choose Dominic as her successor? What is it in his story that made him the likely candidate?

ESSENTIAL QUESTIONS

1. Evey goes through many changes throughout the course of the novel. What changes occurred in her and what were the most significant events that brought them about?
2. V is clearly an intelligent and highly educated man who often uses quotes in his speeches, and his deliveries are constructed in such a way that they come across as being witty. What evidence do you see that V has a sense of humor?
3. What does the novel say about revenge and forgiveness?

4. In what ways is V a hero? Why? Can he also be seen as a villain? Why? Do you think that Alan Moore intentionally instilled him with this ambiguity?

ESSAY TOPICS

1. Do you think that V is a terrorist or freedom fighter? Cite specific details from the novel and support your reasoning with details.
2. What role do women play in the novel? How are they characterized—particularly Evey and Valerie—throughout the novel? What kinds of experiences do they have living in London? How do they contribute to the narrative as a whole? Cite specific details from the novel.
3. Do you think that V's efforts have brought about any significant changes in London? How has society changed because of his actions? Cite specific details from the novel.

PROJECT

BACK TO THE FUTURE

Science fiction stories, such as *V for Vendetta*, fall under the category of speculative fiction, which includes science fiction, fantasy, and horror. Speculative fiction is literature that asks "What if?" What if we could travel among the stars? What if you could fill an object like a ring with pure evil? What if the dead came back to life? One of the main purposes of science fiction—aside from entertainment—is to take problems that we face in our world and put them in a different setting. The goal is to comment on and change the way we think.

Keep in mind, speculative fiction is not always set in the future, is not always technology-based, and the differences between the fictional world and our own are not always that extreme. For years, science fiction writers have imagined what the world will be like. Some writers have imagined it as a utopia (a perfect world) or as a dystopia (a bad or unpleasant world). A story like *V for Vendetta* envisions a dystopic world set in a not-too-distant future that is controlled through violence and fear.

Although the future, much like our current world, will most likely be a combination of both good and bad aspects, what do you imagine the future will be like? Divide yourselves into 12 groups and choose a different aspect of culture to speculate how it will be in the future. The 12 aspects of culture are food, clothing, recreation, government, education, language, religion, transportation, economy, environment, culture, and the arts.

Each group should create a handout that they will give to the other groups. Using the handouts, create a story set in the future using all aspects of the culture. What will the future be like? Use the lines below for brainstorming.

_____

_____

_____

_____

_____

_____

_____

_____

CHAPTER 5

MANGA

**SUGGESTED TIMELINE
1–2 WEEKS**

- History/Osamu Tezuka profile (2–3 days)
- *Metropolis* (1 week)
  - Everybody Knows It's Tough to Grow Up project (2–3 days)

WHAT IS MANGA?

Taken from a Japanese word that means "whimsical drawings," manga is recognized worldwide as comics that originate in Japan. The rise of manga began with U.S. occupation in Japan in the years following World War II from 1945–1952. The U.S. censored any stories that contained prowar or military elements. The G.I.'s in the country brought with them many things that found their way into manga. American comic books, films, and cartoons all had a heavy influence on the manga produced during the 7 years of occupation. U.S. influence can be seen in the work of Osamu Tezuka (2008), particularly in his long-running series, *Tetsuwan Atomu* ("The Mighty Atom," or *Astro Boy* in the U.S.). Astro Boy was a super-powered but naïve robot boy, whose superpowers are strongly reminis-

Look at manga produced during the U.S. occupation of Japan and manga produced after occupation. What differences do you notice?

View *shōnen manga* and *shōjo*. Do you see how they appeal to boys and girls separately? Could they have cross-gender appeal?

cent of Superman. The artwork in the comic is very heavily influenced by Walt Disney's animation style.

In the postoccupation years, manga flourished with a jump in readership. Manga was divided into two genres, one aimed at boys, *shōnen manga*, and one aimed at girls, *shōjo*. Today, *shōnen manga* is geared at young men, and *seinen manga* is for men older than 18 and includes more mature subject matter. *Shōjo* is still for girls of all ages. The stories range from romance stories to female superheroes.

Creator Profile

Osamu Tezuka

Although he has come to be known as the "Godfather of Anime" and the Manga-no-kamisama (the god of manga), Osamu Tezuka began his life as a sensitive boy with an awkward nickname. Called *gashagasha-atama* ("messy head," roughly translated), by his peers he was comforted by his mother, who told him to simply look up at the blue sky, which brought him happiness and confidence.

The oldest of three children, Tezuka regularly attended the Takarazuka Theater with his mother in Takarazuka City, Hyōgo. The theater company was comprised entirely of women, who would play the male roles in drag. They were known for their romantic musicals, and the design of their costumes were a source of inspiration for Tezuka when he became an artist and an animator.

Drawing comics when he was only in his second year of schooling, he assumed the pen name "Osamushi," which he took from a kind of bug because it resembled his own name. His first published works were *Diary of Ma-chan* and *Shin Takarajima* after World War II, which kickstarted the golden age of manga.

Known as the Japanese Walt Disney, Tezuka found inspiration in early Walt Disney features, and the distinctive large eyes that are associated with a lot of manga came from the look of Bambi and Mickey Mouse.

After enduring a childhood illness that made his arms swell, Tezuka felt inspired by the doctor who saved him and considered becoming a doctor. Feeling conflicted, he sought the advice of his mother. When he asked her what he should do, she responded by telling him to do what he enjoys most. Her advice confirmed his original desires, and he continued to work on manga. He went on to create such titles as the long-running *Astro Boy*, *Princess Knight*, *Kimba the White Lion*, and *Phoenix*, an ongoing story of life and death that he worked on until the end of his life.

Not only a writer and artist, Tezuka was also a pioneer in anime. He headed his own animation studio called Mushi Productions. Tezuka continued creating manga and anime until his death from liver cancer in 1989. His innovations in both manga and anime are still seen today, and he has remained an inspiration for many writers and artists.

METROPOLIS

Originally published in 1949, Osamu Tezuka's (2003) *Metropolis* is a legendary early manga and one of the first to garner attention on a large scale. It shares thematic parallels with the 1927 German silent film, although Tezuka claimed to have seen only a single frame from the film at the time that he was producing the manga.

Themes

With ever-rapidly advancing technology, the theme of man versus machine has long been prevalent in pop culture, from John Henry attempting to out-drive the steam hammer to films such as *2001: A Space Odyssey* and *The Terminator* series. The theme permeates throughout the novel. The character of Michi is created as a perfect weapon against humanity to be wielded by a corrupt politician in his quest for world domination.

The question of man's search for identity is central to the story. Although Michi is created for one purpose (i.e., destruction), she befriends a naïve young boy named Ken'ichi, who becomes her best friend and who shows her that although she is a machine, humanity exists within her. Ken'ichi's search for strength to save Michi raises the question of whether she is defined by her original purpose or what she believes herself to be.

The Cold War between the Soviet Union and the United States began at the conclusion of World War II. In the novel, Tezuka explores where his own feelings about the Cold War lie. The look of Metropolis is based on the skyscrapers of many American cities, such as Chicago or New York, but the oppressive and sometimes brutal government mirrors Soviet control under Stalin.

Characters

Dr. Charles Lawton: A scientist hired by the Red Party to create the perfect weapon that would look and appear to be human. Dr. Lawton finds that he is unable to allow his creation to be used as a weapon and decides to flee from the Red Party with Michi.

Discuss

Stylistically, the look of *Metropolis* borrows heavily from both the early work of Walt Disney and the animation of Fleischer Studios. View work from both and discuss the style of *Metropolis*.

RESEARCH AND DISCUSS
Research the Cold War and discuss how it relates to the novel. Tezuka seemed unsure of which side was right. Does he resolve that in the novel? How?

DISCUSS
• Discuss man's search for identity. Do we develop our identities, or are they in some way predetermined?
• Look at several examples of man versus machine. Why is this such an enduring theme? Are the paranoid feelings sometimes associated with rapid advancements in technology valid or not?

Michi: Although she is an android created to be a weapon by the Red Party, she is blissfully unaware of the reasons for her existence.

Ken'ichi: A naïve and kind boy who befriends Michi. He is eventually forced to decide whether he is strong enough to oppose his best friend after she turns on humanity.

Detective Moustachio: A detective searching for Dr. Lawton. After Lawton's death, he helps his nephew Ken'ichi search for Michi's parents.

Duke Red: A corrupt politician who conspires to use Dr. Lawton and his creation, Michi, to rule the world.

Superintendent General Notarlin: The superintendent general of the city's police force. Notarlin stands against the corrupt Duke Red and the Red Party.

Dr. Yorkshire Bell: A scientist who, along with Notarlin, monitors sun spots and radioactivity within the city.

Metropolis

The novel opens in an undisclosed future year with Dr. Bell explaining the evolution and eventual demise of certain creatures, from dinosaurs to the saber-toothed tiger. Although he notes that mankind's intelligence makes him the current dominant species, he wonders whether the day will come when another species will take its place and leave man extinct.

A conference of scientists has been infiltrated by the murderous Red Party and their leader, Duke Red, who is a master of disguise. The major talk of the conference is that the sun has become covered with sunspots. Meanwhile, Dr. Lawton has all but abandoned hope on his 30-year-long project of creating synthetic cells. However, the sunspots irradiate his cells, which give them life. Seizing upon this, Duke Red orders Lawton create a synthetic life form that may be used as a weapon. Fearing the worst, Lawton destroys his lab after accomplishing the task in hopes that Red will be convinced that the android, modeled to look like a little girl, has been destroyed with it.

Now being raised as Lawton's child and unaware of her actual purpose and powers, Michi accidentally knocks out Lawton. Going outside to play, she saves a little girl who is selling violets from being hit by a vehicle. When a mob surrounds Michi, a little boy, Ken'ichi, recognizes her and drags her to a museum to a statue replica of The Angel of Rome. Spotting the android that he believed to have been destroyed, the museum's curator reports the sighting to Duke Red, who pays a visit to Dr. Lawton. Lawton is mortally wounded by Red just as Detective Moustachio arrives. Without an arrest warrant, he is unable to do anything and is forced to let Red and his men go. In his final moments, Lawton shows Moustachio a film about the creation of Michi and her powers.

Returning home, Moustachio finds that his nephew, Ken'ichi, has brought home a new friend, Michi. He leaves Michi to Ken'ichi's trust and goes to police headquarters to seek the advice of Superintendent General Notarlin, who introduces him to Police Inspector Ganimarl of France and Sherlock Holmes of England. Gainmarl and Holmes leave for the museum, where it's been reported that people are being attacked by giant rat creatures (who look suspiciously like Mickey Mouse).

After a car crash caused by the same giant rat creatures, Moustachio stumbles upon the Red Party's lair. He is captured by Red and his men following a failed escape attempt that was aided by a slave robot. Red then reveals his plan to create a chemical weapon and admits that he is responsible for the sunspots. He refers to himself as "Napoleon of the Electronic Age." Red attempts to bargain with Moustachio, offering his freedom in exchange for Michi, which Moustachio refuses.

Michi, now made to look like a boy for protection, begins school with Ken'ichi on the same day as Emmy, the violet-selling little schoolgirl that she saved earlier in the novel. Emmy's schooling is being sponsored by a mysterious old man who is underwriting her education in exchange for luring Michi to her older sister, a gangster. At home, Ken'ichi discovers Dr. Lawton's journal and the true identity of Michi is revealed to him.

Dr. Bell discovers that the mutation in the rats is a result of the sunspots, which is mutating animals, insects, and vegetables. Notarlin reveals that Red is currently disguised as the mysterious old man who is sponsoring Emmy's schooling.

Still at Red headquarters, Moustachio is able to ascertain that Red's chemical weapon has not been used because the headquarters have been overrun with the rat creatures. Using the skin of one that dies, he is able to disguise himself and escape the base.

Emmy's purpose within the school is discovered, and the other children wish to see her expelled. She is saved by Michi and taken to Ken'ichi's house, where Emmy's older sister, the gangster, has arrived, demanding Michi be turned over to them. Ken'ichi is able to hide Michi by using a gender switch on the robot that makes him appear again as a girl, not the boy they were searching for. Soon after, they discover that Michi has run away.

Now free after disguising himself as a rat to escape, Moustachio returns to police headquarters, having figured out that Red has infiltrated the police disguised as legendary British detective, Sherlock Holmes. Notarlin and Ganimarl have been taken captive by Red on his luxury ocean liner. Michi, still disguised as a girl, has stowed away on the ship.

Michi discovers the crew's identity and radios for the police, after which she is caught and identified and told of her true purpose by Red, who turns her back into a boy. Michi snaps and attacks Red and his men. Michi convinces Red's robot

Discuss

The rat creatures attacking people at the museum look very similar to an angry Mickey Mouse. Knowing that Tezuka was inspired by the art of Walt Disney studios, do you think it was a conscious choice on his part? Why would he use such an iconic cartoon as the inspiration for an evil creature?

Discuss

Duke Red is portrayed as a master of disguise, which allows him to infiltrate various places, such as the science convention, school, and police headquarters. Was this a good character choice by Tezuka or a convenient plot device?

RESEARCH AND DISCUSS

The look and powers of Michi inspired another famous Tezuka (2008) creation, *Astro Boy*. Look at an *Astro Boy* manga and compare and contrast the two characters. What similarities and differences exist between the two?

slaves to join him in destroying the ship. In the confusion, Notarlin and Ganimarl escape in time to witness the destruction of the ship and the robots condemning Red and his men to be incinerated. Michi and the robots declare war on humanity and set off toward Metropolis. Notarlin and Ganimarl learn from one of the surviving members of the Red Party that the sunspots, which mutated everything and give power to Michi, are controlled by a radiation emitter. They realize they need to destroy the emitter to save the city.

Following the destruction of the emitter, the pair notify the city of the impending robot attack. Moustachio has the police declare martial law. As Michi and the robots arrive in the city and begin to destroy it, Ken'ichi confronts him on the roof of a skyscraper and attempts to reason with him and convince him to stop. When he is unsuccessful, he attempts to fight Michi but is easily outmatched. When all hope appears lost, Michi begins to smoke and falls from the top of the skyscraper.

As Michi lies dying, Dr. Bell appears on a broadcast and explains to the citizens that Michi was in search of the happiness that would come from knowing who his mother and father were. When it was revealed by Duke Red that he had no mother and father, he snapped and set off on the path of the destruction.

The novel concludes with Dr. Bell once again discussing the possibility of mankind someday becoming extinct.

ESSENTIAL QUESTIONS

1. The story begins with Dr. Bell discussing the evolution of the dominant species on Earth. The book concludes with him theorizing that machines might someday end man's dominance. Is this a real possibility or is humanity's dominance on Earth permanent?
2. Was Michi a completely innocent character that was a victim of fate or to blame for his/her actions at the end of the novel?
3. Who is the hero of *Metropolis* and why?

PROJECT

EVERYBODY KNOWS IT'S TOUGH TO GROW UP

Metropolis has many themes that run throughout it, but one of them is a child's search for identity. Although Michi may be destined to destroy the world, he spends a majority of the book as a confused and often scared child, as we all were at different times in childhood.

Brainstorm about a time in your life when you were searching for your identity. How did you see the world during this crucial stage in your development? Were you trusting of adult guidance? Did you fear growing up? Where did you seek solace from when you were scared? Use the lines below for brainstorming.

After answering these questions, use the memory by recasting it as a story set in a different time period. Childhood is a time when we all first developed an active imagination, which will lend itself to this project. It doesn't have to necessarily be manga-influenced, like *Metropolis*, but simply reimagined in a fictionalized way. Include illustrations throughout the story, so that readers will be able to glimpse into the scary, new world of childhood memory.

_____

_____

_____

_____

_____

_____

_____

_____

_____

_____

_____

_____

CHAPTER 6

FICTION

**SUGGESTED TIMELINE
3–5 WEEKS**

- Intro/Will Eisner profile
  (1–2 days)
- *A Contract With God*
  (1–2 weeks)
  ○ My Neighborhood project
    (2–3 days)
- *The League of Extraordinary
  Gentlemen* (2–3 weeks)
  ○ A Literary Justice League
    project (2–3 days)

COMIC CHARACTERS AREN'T ALWAYS SUPER

As discussed in Chapter 3, comics began dealing with more controversial topics that deviated from the traditional superhero versus supervillain storylines during the 1970s. With the expanding possibilities of the medium, many creators were able to publish personal stories for the first time. The first publishers to specialize in nonsuperhero stories, such as Fantagraphics, started during this time. Dave Sim used his independently published *Cerebus* comics as a platform for the creator's political beliefs. Superhero stories started to tell more mature stories that dealt with real-world issues, such as political corruption and drug abuse.

With the rise in alternative comics that did not focus on superheroes, many creators began to see the possibilities of the medium beyond the parameters that

**RESEARCH
AND DISCUSS**
Research an independent graphic novel publisher. What's the company's history? What are some of the significant works it's published?

had defined it since the creation of Superman. One such creator was Will Eisner, who had made his name working on superhero stories but had grown bored with telling the same overused tales and wanted to create something personal.

Creator Profile

Will Eisner

Although many of the creators who have been profiled throughout this book are legendary in the field of graphic literature for good reasons, none can lay claim to a career as long and as relevant as Will Eisner's. Eisner's career lasted for nearly 70 years from his first published work in 1936 to his final book, *The Plot: The Secret Story of the Protocols of the Elders of Zion*, published shortly before his death in 2005.

Like many of the Golden Age creators, Eisner was born to Jewish immigrants in New York City. His father was an artist who had painted backdrops for various vaudeville and Jewish theaters, and his son showed a similar artistic aptitude. His mother did not see much future in her son pursuing art, but his father encouraged him to pursue his artistic goals while studying business.

In high school, Eisner did illustrations for the yearbook and the school paper. After high school, he briefly attended art school, which led him to a job with *New York American*, a newspaper. He also did freelance illustrations for different pulp magazines.

Eisner's high school friend, Bob Kane (the creator of *Batman*), suggested he submit his work to an early comic book, *Wow, What a Magazine!* He worked on pirate and secret agent strips. In 1939, Eisner created one of his most enduring characters for Quality Comics. *The Spirit* was a syndicated strip that ran in newspapers who wanted a comic to compete with the success of the ever-growing number of superheroes. Eisner was able to negotiate a deal with the distributor that allowed him to keep the rights to his characters, an unheard of thing at the time. The character ran for 12 years, from 1940 through 1952.

While serving in the army during World War II, Eisner developed a comic book that would serve as a teaching tool for soldiers. The comics featured a bumbling, accident-prone soldier named Joe Dope and were written in a language that the soldiers could understand. Working on *Joe Dope*, *Army Motors*, and *Firepower* during the war, and *PS, The Preventative Maintenance Monthly* afterward was one of Eisner's longest running jobs, lasting from 1942 through 1970.

Starting in the 1970s, Eisner was able to move away from superheroes and tell longer, more personal stories in graphic novels. Beginning with the publication of *A Contract With God* (Eisner, 2006/1978), Eisner produced novels in several genres and told many stories focusing on Jews, including the *Contract with God* trilogy and *Fagin the Jew*, which told the story of Oliver Twist's pickpocket teacher and lifted the character above the anti-Semitic portrayal that Eisner felt the character received in the novel.

In addition to his extensive body of work, Eisner wrote two instructional books on creating graphic literature and taught classes on comic art at New York's School of Visual Arts. Known by the end of his career as "the father of graphic novels," Eisner passed away in January of 2005 from complications following open-heart surgery. His legacy can be seen in numerous writers and artists who cite him as an influence and pay tribute to his work, and in the Eisner Awards, the Oscars of comic books, which are handed out every year at San Diego's Comic-Con International.

A CONTRACT WITH GOD

According to Will Eisner, two events led him to create his seminal graphic novel. While attending comic conventions in the early-to-mid-1970s, Eisner met many of his fans who first started reading his work with *The Spirit* in the 1950s, but who were now in their 30s and 40s and were no longer interested in superhero stories. As a result, he set out to create an adult comic.

The other event, which was not revealed until years later, was that Eisner found himself questioning the existence of God after his daughter, like Frimme's daughter in the novel, died after a bout with leukemia. Until this revelation, only Eisner's closest friends even knew that he had a daughter.

Themes

The central theme that runs through all four chapters is faith. The first chapter deals with the faith that we put in God and what is expected from Him in return. Frimme makes a contract with God and is angered at what he perceives to be God's refusal to live up to His end of the contract.

The characters that populate the tenement buildings seem to be trapped in their lives in one way or another and are unable to break free. The decaying urban setting is used as a metaphor for the characters' lives and serves as another recurring theme.

Characters

Frimme Hersh: A Jewish immigrant from Russia who, upon arriving in America, enters into a contract with God that stipulates that Frimme will do God's good work, as long as God blesses his life. When Frimme's daughter dies, he considers the contract void and changes his attitude and becomes a slumlord. Later in his life, he attempts to create another contract with God.

Discuss

- Tenement life is marked by what is known as urban decay. Research and discuss urban decay. Does it add to the plight of the tenants' lives, or are they simply unwilling to try to better their situations?
- Frimme feels that God has not held up His end of the contract and throws it out. If someone enters into such a contract, is he or she truly owed something or is his or her reward that of a good, pious life?

Eddie: An alcoholic singer who sings in the alleys between the tenement buildings. When he is presented with a chance to sing professionally, his demons prevent him from taking advantage of the opportunity.

Opera singer: A former opera singer who recognizes the singer's talent and attempts to give him an opportunity.

Mr. Scuggs: The super at the Dropsie Avenue tenement building. Although he is portrayed as angry and abusive to the tenants, he is actually a lonely, sad man.

Goldie: A receptionist at a textile business who is vacationing at a "cooka-lein" (a type of retreat), a vacation destination for many Jews during the summer, and dreams of meeting a man of a higher social class.

Benny: A conman staying at the retreat who claims to be in the fur business.

Herbie: A socially awkward man who works at Grossman's, a hotel at the cookalein. He is attracted to Goldie but finds his advances rebuffed when she discovers that he works at Grossman's, which she believes makes him beneath her, not knowing that he works as a doctor.

Maralyn Minks: A manipulative woman visiting the resort to get away from her husband.

Irving Minks: The jealous and abusive husband of Maralyn.

Part I: A Contract With God

On a day so rainy that it floods the streets, Frimme Hersh returns home from the funeral of his daughter. Once home, he breaks down crying at the injustice of her death, which he deems unfair because, as a youth, he had made a contract with God.

Frimme grew up in Russia during the reign of Tsar Alexander II at a time when anti-Semitism swept through the country, which resulted in attacks on Jewish communities. As he grew up, he proved himself to be remarkable, kind, loving, and intelligent. He was told often that "God will reward him" for his kind deeds. After another terrible attack on the community that left many people dead, Frimme traveled with a Rabbi to America. On their journey, Frimme asks about the nature of God and decides that he will make a contract with Him. Writing the contract on a small stone, he keeps it in his pocket as he arrives in America.

Once in America, he works hard and studies and becomes a valuable member of his synagogue. He stays true to the contract through his good works. One day, he finds an infant girl abandoned at his front door and decides that it is a part of the contract and adopts the girl. As the child, named Rachelle after his mother, grows, Frimme finds the true joy of his life. The child becomes sick, however, and dies of leukemia.

In the present day, he confronts God and asks why he held up so faithfully his end of the contract, only to have God ignore His. Through a violent storm, he demands answers from God, before finally spitting on the contract and casting it out the window to the street below.

The next day, Frimme shaves off his beard and completely alters his look. Taking bonds from the synagogue that had been entrusted to him, he uses them as collateral and buys the tenement building at Dropsie Avenue, in which he lives.

His first act is to raise the cost of rent for all the tenants. Over time, he becomes so wealthy that he is able to accumulate more property. As he buys and sells real estate, he continues to keep the Dropsie Avenue property. He takes on a mistress and lives what he deems to be a wealthy lifestyle.

One day, he returns to the synagogue and returns the bonds with added interest. He demands that in exchange for the bonds and interest, the elders write him a new contract with God. He recounts for them the history of the previous contract and the circumstances by which it was voided. In exchange for the new contract, he will donate the Dropsie Avenue building to the synagogue.

After much laboring, the elders draw up the contract and present it to Frimme, who gives them the deed to the building. At home, he reads through the contract and is hopeful that his life will return to doing good deeds, getting married, and having another daughter. At that moment, he has a heart attack and dies.

That night, a single bolt of lightning strikes but comes without a storm. The power of the lightning shakes the building and is reminiscent of the night Frimme broke his contract. Later that night, a fire starts and burns down all of the buildings on Dropsie Avenue, save for Frimme's building. A young boy, Shloime Khreks, who saved many people from the fires, is thanked by the people, who tell him that "God will reward him." The next day, some bullies throw rocks at him. As he flees, he picks up one of the rocks and discovers it to be Frimme's original contract. He reads the contract and, taking it as a sign, signs it himself and enters into a contract with God.

It appears that Shloime Khreks was fated to find Frimme's contract. Write a short story with illustrations that follows Shloime after he enters into the same contract. Will he follow the same path or have a happier ending?

ESSENTIAL QUESTIONS

1. Frimme throws his contract with God out of the window, but unlike the tablets of Moses, it does not break. What reason does the contract stay intact?

2. Why is it important that it's raining on the night that Frimme breaks the contract? What is the rain symbolic of?

3. Why does Frimme seek out a second contract with God and what are the consequences of it?

4. Why did Frimme die at the end of this chapter? Was his death inevitable?

Part 2: The Street Singer

During the 1930s, street singers become regular fixtures in the alleys between the tenements. They sing popular songs and parts of operas. The tenants throw money out of their windows to the singers. One night, a note is thrown to one of the singers, inviting him upstairs to one of the apartments.

In the apartment, the singer finds a woman who tells him about how beautiful his singing is. She cooks him food and reveals herself to be a former opera singer whose career was derailed by her husband, who was an abusive alcoholic. She gives the singer money and tells him to buy a suit and clean himself up. After he leaves, the woman calls in a favor at a venue to get the singer a booking.

The singer takes the opera singer's money and uses it to buy whiskey. Returning home, it is revealed that he is married and is an abusive drunk, just like the opera singer's husband was. After hitting his wife and throwing their baby, he apologizes and vows to get better.

The singer goes to a bar and brags about how things are going to turn around for him with the opera singer's help. It is then that he realizes that he does not remember where she lives because he sings in so many alleys that he does not recognize a difference between the buildings. He leaves the bar and returns to singing in alleys.

WRITE AND ILLUSTRATE

As seen with the opera singer and the singer's abused wife, women in the story are portrayed as sad and lonely. Choose one of the novel's female characters and write and illustrate a short story that gives her more depth.

ESSENTIAL QUESTIONS

1. What is the moral lesson of this chapter?
2. Is the singer's failure to capitalize on an opportunity a form of retribution for the ways in which he mirrors the opera singer's husband?

Part 3: The Super

The super at the Dropsie Avenue tenement is an angry man who treats the tenants terribly to keep them afraid. He serves as the middle man between the landlord and the tenants and represents the enemy in that capacity. Because of his position as such, he is a lonely man who must stay isolated in order to maintain his reputation. He lives alone in the basement of the building with his dog as his only friend.

When he goes to check on the hot water in one of the apartments, he discovers the tenant's niece, whom he finds attractive, is visiting her. Later on, he is visited by the young girl, who hits on him. The girl then poisons the super's dog and steals his money. Realizing what has happened, he chases the girl, who threatens to tell people that he hit her. When the tenants respond to the noise, he returns to his dead dog.

The police arrive after the girl's aunt contacts them with false allegations of the super attacking the girl. With the police at his door, the super takes his own life.

ESSENTIAL QUESTIONS

1. What does this chapter say about the nature of lonely people?
2. Is the super destined to be punished for his loneliness and isolation?
3. Is the young girl culpable for her role in the super's death or was she simply taking advantage of a deviant?

> **Discuss**
>
> The story of the super is very brief and leaves parts of the story unanswered. What reasons did the girl have for stealing from the super and killing the dog? Did her aunt have anything to do with it?

Part 4: Cookalein

The story starts in the tenements as several of the residents prepare to leave for summer vacations at the Cookalein retreat. Goldie, a receptionist at a fur business, dreams of meeting a man who will take her away from her life.

Upon her arrival, Goldie meets two men: Herbie, an awkward man who works at the retreat, and Benny, a charming conman who claims to work in the fur business. Feeling that Herbie is beneath her, Goldie rebuffs his advances and seeks out Benny.

Two subplots are presented in tandem about infidelity. In the first, a man cheats on his wife with a beautiful, blonde woman. She asks him to leave his wife, but he tells her that he can't because his wife is ill and they have children to raise. When he returns to his wife later, she reveals that she knows that he has been cheating on her but that she will never grant him a divorce. In the second story, a woman vacationing alone cheats on her husband with a young man who works at the retreat. When she is caught by her husband, he beats her in front of the traumatized young man. The couple leaves together with her professing her love for her husband.

Goldie and Benny meet in the woods behind the resort. Benny attempts to seduce Goldie, but she refuses his advances, wanting respect and love first. It is then revealed that both of them lied about their backgrounds and were using their lies to move up into a higher social class. Angered by the truth about Goldie, he sexually assaults her.

When she returns to the resort, she seeks out Herbie and tells him what happened to her in the woods. Herbie finds Benny and threatens him, and it is revealed through their conversation that Herbie is a doctor. Herbie agrees to stay

The characters in the fourth story all go to the same vacation spot every summer. Write about a place your family visited regularly and your memories of those trips.

quiet because he's intimidated by Benny, and Benny returns his attention to a woman he has been flirting with.

Back in the city, Goldie announces to her coworkers that she is getting married to a doctor. Benny tells a friend that he is going to marry a girl whose father works in the diamond business.

ESSENTIAL QUESTIONS

1. How does poverty affect the lives of the characters in this chapter?
2. Why is infidelity so prevalent in this chapter? Is it part of the characters' desires to escape their lives?
3. Many of the characters are portrayed as being manipulative or morally corrupt. Why is Herbie the only one who is presented as being somewhat virtuous?
4. What do the characters in each of the stories have in common? What links each of the four narratives?
5. What is the underlying philosophy about God in each of the stories?
6. What do the stories say about tenement living during this time?

ESSAY TOPICS

1. In the first chapter, Frimme feels that God has failed to live up to their contract. Using Frimme's story as the central focus, explore the idea of the covenant that exists between man and God and what, if anything, we are owed in return for doing good work and living honest lives.
2. Characters in each of the first three chapters have a tragic flaw that leads to their downfall. Compare and contrast two of the characters and discuss whether each is a victim of circumstance or whether he is to blame for his respective fall.

PROJECT

MY NEIGHBORHOOD

Everyone has memories of the neighborhood in which they grew up. Those memories might be of summer nights playing hide-and-seek with the neighbors, or perhaps of a neighbor of whom everyone was afraid. These stories from our childhoods fill up our minds, creating a mythology of youth that can evoke so many different emotions.

Brainstorm different stories of your childhood neighborhood. Perhaps they are of things that happened to you personally or just a story you heard from a friend or family member. Select four of these stories to develop into a project set in the neighborhood. You may choose to make all of the stories be in some way about yourself or you may not be present at all; the decision is up to you.

For each story, include illustrations. If you aren't comfortable with attempting the art, then use photographs or images from the Internet.

Where did you live? _____

_____

Who were your neighbors? _____

_____

_____

Who were your friends? _____

_____

_____

List your favorite memories. _____

_____

_____

_____

_____

THE LEAGUE OF EXTRAORDINARY GENTLEMEN

Created by DC Comics editor Sheldon Mayer and writer Gardner Fox, the *Justice Society of America* was the first superhero team ever created. Although the idea of heroes teaming up was not a new idea, it was certainly a new concept for comic books. Not only did it allow readers to see all of their favorite heroes in one comic, it also introduced the idea that they all inhabited the same universe. In the wake of the individual books' success, other superhero team books began to appear, such as the *Justice League of America*, *The Avengers*, *The Fantastic Four*, and *X-Men*.

With *The League of Extraordinary Gentlemen*, Alan Moore (2002) took the same concept of the superhero team and applied it to literature, choosing characters from Victorian-era novels. He also decided to use primarily characters created by British authors on the team; however, he did use characters created by authors of different nationalities in supporting roles throughout the novel. In addition to the characters on the team, Moore peppered the series with allusions to numerous other characters from other novels and created characters who were ancestors of other famous literary characters, such as Campion Bond, the grandfather of James Bond.

Prereading Project: Character Biographies

Part of reading and appreciating *The League of Extraordinary Gentlemen* lies with the reader not only recognizing but having thorough knowledge of the various characters who populate the book. Although many students might be peripherally familiar with characters such as the Invisible Man or Dr. Jekyll and Mr. Hyde, they may not be as familiar with Captain Nemo or Allan Quatermain. As a prereading project, have students gather into small groups and choose one of the novel's main characters to research and create a character biography. Each group will make a presentation to the class and then hang up its presentation in the classroom for classmates to reference throughout the book.

Themes

Redemption is the overriding theme of the novel. Many of the characters are past their prime and are searching for redemption. Dr. Jekyll, like the Incredible Hulk (a character he partly inspired), is still trying to come to terms with his own dual nature, the beast that lives inside him. Quatermain, the Great White Hunter, is at the end of his life and seeking one last adventure. Wilhelmina Murray (for-

WATCH

View portions of *The Avengers* (Fiege & Whedon, 2012) and *X-Men: First Class* (Goodman, Kinberg, Shuler Donner, Singer, & Vaughn, 2011).

DISCUSS

Discuss the conventions of the superhero team. What are the advantages and disadvantages of such teams?

Discuss

In the 2003 film adaptation of *The League of Extraordinary Gentlemen* (Albert & Norrington, 2003), Tom Sawyer, a U.S. Secret Agent, joined the League as the lone American member, even though Moore's books contain mainly British characters from the Victorian era. Do you agree with Moore's decision to use mainly British characters in the major roles, or do you believe he should have expanded the universe's mythology to be more inclusive of other nationalities?

merly Wilhelmina Harkin in Bram Stoker's novel) seems to be distancing herself from her past. All of the League's characters want redemption but only a few are able to achieve it.

Characters

Campion Bond: The grandfather of Ian Fleming's James Bond. He is the handler of the late 19th-century League team.

The Doctor/Fu Manchu: The main character of Sax Rohmer's (1913/2002) *The Mystery of Dr. Fu Manchu*. Fu Manchu is Professor Moriarty's chief rival and the leader of Chinese organized crime. He is never actually mentioned by name as "Fu Manchu" but instead as "The Doctor" due to copyright laws.

Hawley Griffin: The titular character of H. G. Wells' (1897/2012) *The Invisible Man*. Griffin is depicted as being a sociopath and a traitor.

Edward Hyde/Henry Jekyll: The dueling personalities from Robert Louis Stevenson's (1886/1991) *Strange Case of Dr. Jekyll and Mr. Hyde*. Both men are members of the League, with Jekyll being meek and Hyde being large and evil.

Professor James Moriarty: The "Napoleon of Crime" and the archenemy of Sherlock Holmes from Arthur Conan Doyle's (1893/2012) *The Adventure of the Final Problem*. Moriarty is a personal and professional rival to Dr. Fu Manchu and acts as the head of MI5, Britain's security and internal counterintelligence agency.

Wilhelmina Murray: One of the protagonists of Bram Stoker's (1897/2000) *Dracula*. She is now the leader of the 19th-century Victorian League.

Captain Nemo: The son of an Indian Raja, Nemo appeared in two different Jules Verne novels, *20,000 Leagues Under the Sea* (1870/2006) and *The Mysterious Island* (1874/1988). Nemo is a mysterious antihero, a brilliant scientist, and the captain of a submarine called *Nautilus*.

Allan Quatermain: The Great White Hunter from H. Rider Haggard's (1885/2008) *King Solomon's Mines*. Haggard, through various prequels and sequels, told Quatermain's story from the age of 18 until 68; he is in his late 60s when he joins the League.

Chapter 1: Empire Dreams

At the behest of MI5, Campion Bond recruits Wilhelmina Murray to assemble the League. Escorted by a sea captain who is later revealed to be Captain Nemo, she is sent to Egypt to recruit Allan Quatermain, whom she discovers to be an opium addict and a shell of his former self.

As the duo leave, they are attacked by a group of Arabs who attempt to rape Wilhelmina but are rescued by the arrival of Captain Nemo in his submarine, *Nautilus*. They depart for France to meet with C. Auguste Dupin, the detective in Edgar Allan Poe's "The Murders in the Rue Morgue. They attempt to capture a beast-man who is revealed to be the villainous Mr. Hyde, the alter ego of Dr. Jekyll.

ESSENTIAL QUESTIONS

1. Upon their first meeting, Campion Bond refers to Wilhelmina Murray only by her first name but is quickly corrected and told to refer to her as Miss Murray. Why does Bond feel that he is allowed to call her by her first name in such a familiar way, and is he breaking a social convention in doing so?
2. How has Quatermain fallen into such a life of disrepair? Should someone who is a drug addict be trusted in his current capacity?

Chapter 2: Ghosts and Miracles

After a fight with Mr. Hyde, the trio is able to capture him. After turning him over to MI5, they leave for an all-girls' school in Edmonton to investigate rumors that many of the girls have been impregnated by the Holy Spirit. Upon their arrival, they discover the mysterious "Holy Spirit" is none other than Hawley Griffin, the Invisible Man of H. G. Wells's novel. Griffin, portrayed by Wells as being a psychopath, is now a perverted sociopath.

ESSENTIAL QUESTION

The League has now recruited a drug addict (Quatermain), a monster (Mr. Hyde), and a perverted sociopath. Why do you believe they are populating the League with dangerous or potentially unreliable characters?

Chapter 3: Mysteries of the East

With the team now assembled, Bond reveals that Britain had planned to land a man on the moon but their plan was thwarted by The Doctor. The Doctor has stolen cavorite, the alloy from H. G. Wells' (1901/2000) *The First Men in the Moon*, and plans on using it to gain revenge against Britain.

The League, minus Nemo, who stays aboard the *Nautilus*, leaves for the Limehouse district to investigate. Miss Murray and Griffin attempt to gather information while Quatermain and Jekyll infiltrate The Doctor's hideout. Although they are nearly discovered, they are able to escape.

Back aboard the *Nautilus*, the League pieces together the information they've gathered. Miss Murray believes The Doctor's theft of the cavorite is a part of a larger plan for revenge. They decide to break into his hideout once more to try to recover the alloy.

> **RESEARCH AND DISCUSS**
> Cavorite was introduced in H. G. Wells' (1901/2000) novel *The First Men in the Moon*. Research how the substance is introduced in the novel. What power does it hold?

ESSENTIAL QUESTIONS

1. The senior members of the League, Miss Murray and Quatermain, are each paired with two of the more unstable/untrustworthy members—Griffin and Jekyll. Are these the best pairings of League members? How might the events in this chapter have been different if the pairings had been Miss Murray and Quatermain and Griffin and Jekyll?
2. Nemo routinely stays behind on the *Nautilus* while the others go out on missions. What reasons might he have for not accompanying the League?

Chapter 4: Gods of Annihilation

Quatermain and Miss Murray are able to infiltrate The Doctor's hideout, where they discover a large and armed flying craft. As they are about to be discovered by a guard, an unseen Griffin kills him. Quatermain uses the guard's uniform to sneak inside the craft undetected to recover the cavorite. Griffin brings Jekyll into the hideout and annoys him on purpose to instigate his transformation until he turns into Mr. Hyde, which results in Hyde killing many of The Doctor's henchmen.

The pair escapes into a tunnel, where they become trapped. Realizing that they will be killed by The Doctor's men, the rest of the League all climb on Hyde and escape after Quatermain shoots a hole in the tunnel using his elephant gun. Miss Murray activates the cavorite, allowing the group to fly away.

Back aboard the *Nautilus*, Bond takes the cavorite from the group and congratulates them on a job well done, before leaving to take it back to his boss, M. After he leaves, Griffin follows him undetected and discovers that the mysterious M is actually Sherlock Holmes' arch enemy, Professor James Moriarty.

ESSENTIAL QUESTIONS

In traditional superhero team comic books, it is an unspoken rule that the good guys do not kill villains under any circumstances. Griffin kills one of the Doctor's guards and Hyde kills many of his men. Do you agree with this decision and departure from the superhero comic books on which the League was modeled?

Chapter 5: "Some Deep, Organizing Power"

In a flashback, it is revealed how Moriarty, who was presumed dead in Sir Arthur Conan Doyle's (1893/1992) Sherlock Holmes story *The Adventure of the Final Problem*, managed to live. It is also revealed that he has been in the employ of the British secret service and his criminal empire was nothing more than a front.

Griffin returns to the *Nautilus* and reveals M's true identity. Nemo ascertains that Moriarty plans on using his own flying machine to bomb London's East End in a campaign to destroy The Doctor's criminal empire. The group takes off to stop Moriarty using a hot air balloon that Nemo had aboard the Nautilus.

ESSENTIAL QUESTIONS

Moriarty's plan is to destroy The Doctor's criminal operation, but in the process he would destroy the lives of many innocent people. Is he justified in his actions or is there another way? Explain why or why not.

Chapter 6: The Day of Be-With-Us

The League set out to stop Moriarty's plan, but while the others fight, Griffin strips naked and hides by the ship to avoid having to help in the battle. Quatermain is able to kill many of Moriarty's men before Moriarty is able to disarm him. As Moriarty is about to kill Quatermain, Miss Murray destroys the case containing the cavorite, which Moriarty grabs as he's propelled into the night.

With the battle over, the League returns to the Nautilus, where they are congratulated by Mycroft Holmes (the brother of Sherlock Holmes), who will be replacing Moriarty as the new head of the League.

ESSENTIAL QUESTIONS

Do you see Griffin's refusal to fight as an act of betrayal or simply cowardice? Why?

PROJECT

A LITERARY JUSTICE LEAGUE

Alan Moore's original concept for the *League of Extraordinary Gentlemen* was for it to be a "Justice League in Victorian England." Taking a cue from this concept, choose a different time period in literature and create a "superhero team" of the characters from various novels set during that time. You will need to decide on the team's members and the villain they will face. Fill out the chart below and use the information to develop the story.

MEMBER	LITERARY ORIGIN	ROLE ON THE TEAM

VILLAIN	LITERARY ORIGIN	EVIL PLAN

CHAPTER 7

BIOGRAPHY AND MEMOIR

SUGGESTED TIMELINE 3–4 WEEKS

- History/Art Spiegelman profile (1–2 days)
- Allegories and fables prereading (1–2 days)
- Holocaust research (1–2 days)
- *Maus* (2–3 weeks)
  - History Through Your Family project (2–3 days)

A LIFE IN COMICS

Beginning in the 1970s, many artists used the medium to tell their own stories. In 1972, Justin Green (1972/2009) produced a comic called *Binky Brown Meets the Holy Virgin Mary*, which told the story of his background as a Catholic and a Jew, as well as his battles with Obsessive-Compulsive Disorder. Most notably, writer Harvey Pekar (2003) based his entire career around telling his life story, detailing his life as a file clerk in *American Splendor*. The book was illustrated over the years by a variety of artists.

READ AND DISCUSS

Look at other autobiographical graphic novels, such as Harvey Pekar's (2003) *American Splendor* or Joe Kubert's (2011) *Yossel*. How does each creator use images to convey truths about his life that simple words could not?

Art Spiegelman

Born in Sweden as Itzhak Avraham ben Zev in 1948, Art Spiegelman came to America with his parents as a child in 1951 and was given the name Arthur Isadore, later Art. Growing up with an interest in in art, Art rejected his parents' desire to see him enter a more financially secure field so that he may study art and philosophy at Harpur College from 1965–1968. His collegiate career was cut short when he suffered a nervous breakdown and was institutionalized for a month. His release was met with sadness, as his mother committed suicide a short while later.

In 1969, he got his first job as an illustrator, working freelance for several men's magazines. In the 1970s, Spiegelman began working in underground comics. When the opportunity to produce a strip for Justin Green's *Funny Animals* came about, he had the idea to produce a strip that focused on racism with African Americans being portrayed as mice and Ku Klux Klan members as cats. He eventually rethought the idea and recast it during the Holocaust, an idea that resulted in his most famous work.

Working with his wife, Françoise Mouly, Spiegelman began producing an independent magazine called *Raw* in July of 1980. Along with serializing *Maus* one chapter at a time, the magazine was used as a vessel for showcasing new talent, such as Chris Ware and Gary Panter.

In 1985, Spiegelman learned that Steven Spielberg was producing an animated film about Jewish mice that flee persecution in Europe and come to America. Spiegelman returned to work on *Maus* so that he might get it published before the release of *An American Tail*. Eventually, Pantheon published the first six chapters as *Maus: A Survivor's Tale* with the subtitle *My Father Bleeds History*. The second part of the book, *Maus II: And Here My Troubles Began* followed a few years later.

After the success of *Maus*, Spiegelman worked as an illustrator for *The New Yorker* until 2003. His most famous work came toward the end of his tenure, when he produced what initially appeared to be an all-black cover following the September 11th attacks, but on closer inspection actually featured the World Trade Center towers in silhouette. After leaving the magazine, Spiegelman released *In the Shadow of No Towers* (2004) a few years after the attacks. .

MAUS

Many of us know the story of the Tortoise and the Hare. The cocky Hare, feeling that victory was assured, got lazy and took a nap on the side of the road, which allowed the Tortoise, who moves at a slow and steady pace, to win. As children, we take away from this story that slow and steady wins the race, and it is to the turtle we assign the image of consistency and a well-thought-out plan.

Animals are often seen as symbolic. With birds, we associate the owl with wisdom, the eagle with freedom, and the dove with peace. In snakes, we see deceptiveness, and in the horse, we see nobility. Over time, we assign to these animals a meaning beyond simply what they are but what they represent. Many stories have been told using people, places, and things that are meant to represent something more. It is through the use of symbolic figures that we get the allegory, which is an extended metaphor that uses such symbols to convey an idea or a message to the audience in a simple way.

Wanting to convey his feelings about the Russian Revolution, Stalin's rise to power, and the corruption that resulted from it, George Orwell (1945/1996) wrote the novel *Animal Farm*, which tells the story of a group of abused farm animals that overthrow the farmer and take control of the farm. However noble their intentions, the pigs, who establish themselves as the leaders, take advantage of their power and things quickly become worse than they had ever been under their former drunken and abusive ruler.

In looking for a symbolic way to address racism, Art Spiegelman hit upon the idea of using the relationship between cats and mice, using cats as a way to represent the aggression of racist groups like the Ku Klux Klan (his original plan was for it to be about African Americans), while the fearful and oppressed group would be represented by mice, forced to run and hide for safety whenever the cat is on patrol. It is through this recognizable dynamic of the cat and the mouse that we are able to understand a deeper meaning about the experiences of Jews in Europe during the Holocaust and the nature of hate.

READ AND DISCUSS

View other famous allegories and discuss the message they convey, such as Orwell's (1945/1996) *Animal Farm* or *Grimm's Complete Fairy Tales* (Grimm & Grimm, 1812/2011). How effectively did the author use allegory to convey his or her message?

DISCUSS

Besides the animals discussed in this section, what other animals are recognized as being symbolic of something else? How were they ascribed this meaning?

Themes

Every character in *Maus* lives with guilt of some kind. Vladek, Art's father, feels guilt for the lives lost and the sacrifices that were made to survive the Holocaust. The largest amount of guilt, however, is carried by Art. His older brother, Richieu, whom he never knew, died in the Holocaust and stands as such the perfect sibling that Art feels an intense rivalry with him, despite never having known him.

Although the racism exhibited throughout the novel is depicted as coming from the Germans, as well as the Poles who persecute the Jews as a means of their own survival, Vladek himself is also racist. While decrying the persecution that he faced at German hands, he becomes angered when Art's wife picks up an African American hitchhiker, who he feels is beneath him.

Prereading Research: The Holocaust

Before beginning to read the novel, have students research different aspects of the Holocaust, such as events that led up to it or what happened at different concentration camps, and give presentations to the class to expand their knowledge.

Write

Write about something you felt guilty about and what you did to make amends for your mistake.

- What were the significant events that led to the Holocaust?
- How did it worsen?
- What were the various camps?
- When was each liberated?

Use the reports to make a timeline of the Holocaust in class.

Characters

Art Spiegelman: Art is a cartoonist and has a strained relationship with his father. The thrust of the narrative is his attempt to understand his father's experiences in the Holocaust and how they made his father who he is.

Vladek Spiegelman: Art's father. He is a Polish Jew and a survivor of the Holocaust who came to America in the early 1950s. His experiences have left him nearly obsessive-compulsive, bitter, and anxious. Although he has a clear understanding of the racism he faced as a Jew, he seems completely unaware of how he treats other races now.

Discuss

Although the Jews are portrayed as mice and the Germans as cats, they are not the only animals to appear in the story. What other animals did Spiegelman choose to portray other characters? Why did he choose those animals? What does it say about them?

Anja Spiegelman: Art's mother. She was also a survivor of the Holocaust. She had a nervous breakdown shortly after giving birth to their first child, who did not survive the war, and later committed suicide in 1968.

Mala Spiegelman: Also a survivor of the Holocaust. She is Vladek's second wife, following Anja's suicide. Despite sharing the same experiences, Vladek treats her poorly as a constant reminder that she will never replace Anja in his heart.

Françoise Mouly: Art's wife. She is French but converted to Judaism to please his father.

BOOK 1: MY FATHER BLEEDS HISTORY

Prologue

The novel opens with Art remembering a day when he was rollerskating with his friends. He fell and hurt himself, and his friends laughed at him and left him behind. Upon returning home, he finds his father outside working. When he asks

Art why he's crying, Art tells what his friends did, and his father tells him that if he locked them in a room together without food for a week that he would see what friends really are.

ESSENTIAL QUESTION

Vladek's statement about friends is cryptic. What does it reveal about his experiences and how he feels about human nature?

Part I: The Sheik

Art is visiting his father at his home in Rego Park in Queens, NY. They are not close, and it has been 2 years since they last saw each other. Art's mother, Anja, committed suicide some years earlier, and his father is now remarried to Mala, also a survivor of the Holocaust. Art explains to his father that he wants to write a book about his experiences before and during the Holocaust. His father seems reluctant to talk about it but relents and begins to tell his story.

During the early 1930s, Vladek lived in Częstochowa, Poland, near the German border. He worked in the textile industry and was dating a woman named Lucia. While visiting his family in Sosnowiec in December of 1935, he meets Anja, a girl from a good family. Despite living a long distance apart, the two begin a relationship, talking by phone once a week. Eventually, Anja sends Vladek a picture of herself that he puts on his dresser. When Lucia sees the picture, she ends their relationship.

By the end of 1936, Vladek and Anja are engaged. As Vladek prepares to move to Sosnowiec, Lucia comes to his apartment and begs him to take her back. He refuses and does not hear from her again, but he suddenly stops hearing from Anja, as well. When he contacts her mother, he discovers that she received a letter claiming he only wants to marry her for her money. Vladek travels to see her and discovers that the letter was from Lucia. He convinces Anja to go through with the marriage, and the two are wed in 1937 and move into an apartment owned by her father. Vladek then begins working for her father's hosiery business.

Why is this chapter called "The Sheik?"

ESSENTIAL QUESTIONS

1. What do you notice about Art's relationship with his father that would explain why it has been 2 years since they last saw each other?
2. How does Vladek treat Mala? What does it say about their relationship?

3. As Vladek gets on his exercise bike, we see that he has numbers tattooed on his left fore-arm. What does this image say?

Part 2: The Honeymoon

Returning to visit his father, Art finds him sorting his pills. He takes a total of 30 different pills every day for a variety of reasons but dismisses them as "junk food." The two then sit down to continue Vladek's story.

Prior to meeting and dating Vladek, Anja had a boyfriend who was a communist. For a time, she decoded messages for him but hid the messages with her neighbor, a seamstress, after getting word that the police were coming to search her apartment. The neighbor is arrested during the police search and spends 3 months in jail before being released due to lack of evidence. Vladek is angered at this news and threatens to end their marriage before Anja promises to never again consort with communists.

Anja's father gives Vladek a factory to run so that he may make a good living and take care of his daughter. They have their first child, Richieu, in 1937, but Anja becomes depressed following the birth and soon leaves to stay at a sanitarium in Czechoslovakia. On the train ride through Germany, they see flags with swastikas on them and hear the first rumblings of rampant anti-Semitism in the country.

The sanitarium proves helpful, and Vladek and Anja return home after 3 months and settle into a two-bedroom apartment. They get word that in their absence, the factory was robbed. Anja's father does not suspect any anti-Semitic motivation behind the robbery, though. They set up another factory but within a few months, anti-Semitic riots begin occurring as the Nazis create problems in Poland for the Jews. Anja offends her Polish nurse by implying that Polish people are easily manipulated, which hurts the nurse because she considers them to be family.

By 1939, Vladek receives a letter notifying him that he has been drafted into the military and is sent to the German front.

What early signs do we see that foreshadow future events in the story? How do the characters react to them?

ESSENTIAL QUESTIONS

1. What does Vladek's attitude toward his medication tell you about his feelings on survival?
2. Art Spiegelman uses the swastika throughout the book as an ever-present reminder of the German menace and the impending dangers of their rise to power. How does it come to represent the plight of the Jews in Europe during the war?

Part 3: Prisoner of War

On his next visit, Art and Vladek eat together, and his father insists that he eat everything on his plate, just as when he was a child. Continuing his story, Vladek recounts that when he was 21, his father starved him so that he would fail his army physical. His plan worked for the time being, but Vladek joined the army a year later.

Fighting on the German front, Vladek is captured by the Nazis after he kills a German soldier. He is forced to carry the bodies of Germans to be buried. The Jewish prisoners are made to live outside in tents and are given only small scraps of bread to eat, and the Polish soldiers are allowed to live in heated cabins and are fed twice a day.

Despite the frigid temperatures, Art bathes in a river every day to fend off the lice that have overtaken many of his fellow soldiers. When the opportunity is given to receive better accommodations and more food from the Germans in exchange for labor, Vladek takes the work, which is hard labor work clearing rocks. Although he is able to do the work, many of his fellow soldiers are old and weak and are unable to continue.

One evening, Vladek dreams of his grandfather, who promises him that he will be released from the camp on Parshas Truma, a week occurring once a year in the Jewish calendar. Speaking with a rabbi in the camp, he learns that the next one is to occur in February, which is in 3 months.

Just as his dream prophesized, he is released on Parshas Truma but is put on a train and sent to another camp, where it is rumored that 600 Jews on the last train were taken into the woods and killed. The Jewish leaders of the camps have been able to bribe the Nazi officers into releasing prisoners to nearby family members. Vladek is to be released to his cousin but not before nearly being shot by a German officer when he leaves his tent one evening to use the restroom. He is without his papers when he gets on the train, and by pretending to Polish is able to hide from the Germans.

Upon his release, he is reunited with his parents and finds that his mother is very sick and will not live long. His father, who is very religious, was forced by the Nazis to shave his beard. He is then reunited with his wife and young son.

RESEARCH AND DISCUSS

In this chapter, we see characters wearing masks. Research and discuss the use of masks by different cultures. What functions did they serve? What function do they serve in this chapter?

ESSENTIAL QUESTIONS

1. Vladek's father is shown earlier in the chapter with a beard and wearing a kippah but is without them later in the chapter when he is reunited with his son. What effect does the forced removal of both have on his father?

2. What effect does the killing of the German soldier have on Vladek?

3. Given the allegorical portrayal of all of the characters, how is Vladek able to "disguise" himself as being Polish?
4. What do the different characterizations of the races and ethnicities say about how they are to be viewed by the reader?

Part 4: The Noose Tightens

Art returns to his father's home to find him upset that he didn't arrive earlier to help him fix a drain pipe on the roof. Art purchased a new tape recorder for $75 to help with recording his father's story, but his father admonishes him for not getting a better deal.

Vladek picks up his story where he left off. It is now 1940, and Anja's father's home now houses 12 people. The Germans are controlling the food distribution, although her father is able to get more food for the family through his connections. By this point, all Jewish-owned businesses have been closed by the Nazis. Vladek meets with a former customer, Mr. Ilzecki, who is still in business making uniforms, and they make an arrangement in which Vladek will provide him with cloth in exchange for cash.

After barely escaping during a German raid, Anja's father is able to acquire a priority work card for Vladek, so that he will not be arrested as the German menace increases and the situation begins to turn dire. While taking clothes to Mr. Ilzecki one day, Vladek sees a group of German officers beating Jews with clubs and forcing them onto a train. He is saved from the raid by Mr. Ilzecki, who pulls him into his home. He tells Vladek that the situation is getting worse and that he is sending his son away to stay with a Polish family and recommends that he and Anja do the same with Richieu.

By 1942, all of the remaining Jews have been moved to one section of the town and Vladek and Anja's family now share a small, cramped space. Anja spends her days cleaning and writing about her experiences in a diary. Vladek continues doing business illegally until one of his customers is killed by the Nazis, which leaves him scared to leave his house.

As the situation continues to worsen, all Jews over the age of 70 are sent to a new location to be cared for. Anja's grandparents, both in their 90s, are afraid to go, and the family hides them. When Anja's father is arrested, he sends a note saying that if they don't give up the grandparents, that the Germans will come and arrest more members of the family. After complying with the order, the grandparents are immediately sent to the gas chamber at Auschwitz.

Eventually, the Jews are told to go to a stadium for registration. Fearing what might happen if they fail to appear, 25,000–30,000 Jews come to the stadium to find that they are being divided after registration. The elderly, people without work cards, and anyone with a large number of children are sent to the left side of the stadium, while everyone else is sent to the right. Vladek and most of Anja's family are sent to the right, but when Anja's younger sister, Fela, and her children approach, she is told that she has too many children and is sent to the left. Anja's father sees this and sneaks to the other side of the stadium to be with his daughter. None of them are ever seen again, along with 10,000 other Jews.

In the present, Vladek has grown tired and decides to take a nap. Art leaves him to his nap and goes into the kitchen and speaks with Mala, who is playing solitaire. She shares some of her experiences during the Holocaust with him, including stories of Jews being so tightly packed together in cells that some suffocated. Art asks for help finding his mother's diaries. They are unable to find them amongst his father's things, and Art decides to leave, which upsets Mala who insists that he put everything back as it was so as to not anger his father.

READ AND DISCUSS

We learn that Anja kept a diary about her experiences. Read excerpts from *The Diary of a Young Girl* (Frank, 1947/1993) and discuss them. How is Anne able to remain hopeful, even in the face of a dark future?

ESSENTIAL QUESTION

During the German raid that Vladek witnesses, he is depicted in a single panel surrounded by a Star of David. How does this image serve as a metaphor for Vladek's situation?

Part 5: Mouse Holes

Early one morning, Art receives a frantic phone call from Mala, asking for him to come to the house to help his father, who has climbed onto the roof to fix the drain pipe. Vladek takes the phone and asks Art to come help him but is told by his son that he will call him later. After hanging up, Art tells his wife that he hated helping his father when he was younger because he was always told that what he did was not good enough.

When he calls his father back later, Vladek tells him that he got his neighbor to help. Feeling guilty, Art visits his father a week later and finds him in the garage sorting nails, clearly annoyed. He goes inside and is told by Mala that his father found out about a comic that Art had drawn called "Prisoner on the Hell Planet" that was about his mother's suicide in 1968. Art was living with his parents following a time in a mental hospital. He returned home one day to find that his mother had taken her own life and his father was destroyed. Overcome with guilt, Art remembers the last time he spoke with his mother. She asked him whether he loved her or not, and he responded with, "Sure." Vladek comes into the kitchen and admits that the comic didn't anger him but made him sad. They leave together to go to the bank, and on their walk, Vladek continues his story.

With all of the Jews being taken out of Sosnowiec and sent to a ghetto in the nearby town of Srodula, Vladek and Anja decide to send their young son to live with her sister and her family in Zawiercie, where they might be kept safe. A short while later, when the Nazis begin rounding up all of the Jews in Zawiercie, her sister poisons herself and the children, which Vladek and Anja don't discover until sometime later.

As the Nazis begin rounding up Jews in Srodula, Vladek protects his family by building a hiding place within a coal bin where they can hide during the raids. Later, after moving to a different house, they build a similar hideout in an attic. They are seen one night by a fellow Jew who claims that he is looking for food. Although they briefly consider killing him to protect themselves, they ultimately left him go. The next day, the Nazis come and arrest them and take them to a secured area within the ghetto, which is a waiting area for Auschwitz.

In a desperate move, Vladek seeks the help of his cousin, Haskel, who is a Chief of Jew Police. After giving him a diamond ring, he is able to get himself and Anja released. When Anja's parents attempt to make a similar deal, Haskel does not help them, and they are sent to Auschwitz. Haskel is well connected, and is able to secure work for Vladek repairing shoes for German soldiers.

As more Jews are sent from Srodula to Auschwitz, Haskel arranges to be smuggled out of the ghetto. His two brothers create a hiding spot in the shoe factory. Vladek and Anja finally learn of Richieu's death, and are overcome with grief, Anja tells Vladek that she wants to die. He tells her that death would be too easy and that they must struggle to live and can do it together.

After much time in the hideout, the 15 people run out of food and become desperate. Haskel's brother, Pesach, tells everyone that he has made a deal with the guards to let them escape the ghetto. Vladek and Anja decide to stay because they don't trust the Germans. The next morning, the rest are shot by the Germans as they escape. After the ghetto is completely evacuated, Vladek and Anja leave together to Sosnowiec.

In present day, at the bank, Vladek gives Art a key to his safe-deposit box where he has kept his valuables from before the war. He laments to Art that he wishes he had never remarried because he doesn't trust Mala and feels that she is only after his money.

Part 5 presents Art's real comic, *Prisoner on the Hell Planet* being incorporated into the story. What imagery does he use to tell his story?

ESSENTIAL QUESTIONS

1. This chapter begins to play up the idea of the Jews as mice. What metaphors, including the chapter's title, are used to accomplish this?
2. Why does Art portray himself as a prisoner in his comic with regard to his mother's suicide?

3. As the situation becomes more desperate, Vladek's love and care for Anja increases as they struggle to survive. How does his concern for Anja stand in stark contrast for how he treats Mala now?

Part 6: Mouse Trap

Art finds Mala crying in the kitchen. She is upset because she feels that Vladek treats her like a maid, providing her with only $50 a month while he stashes hundreds of thousands of dollars. She uses her own savings to provide for the household. Art feels that his experiences during the Holocaust made him be the way he is, but Mala knows other survivors, none of which act like Vladek. Art is concerned that his portrayal of his father comes across like a racist Jewish stereotype.

Vladek joins them in the kitchen, and Art shows him his early work on the book. Both Mala and Vladek feel that the book will be something special. Mala and Vladek get into an argument about her trips to a hairdresser, and Vladek confides to Art that she constantly threatens to leave him. Father and son go outside to the garage to continue talking.

In 1944, Vladek and Anja have returned to Sosnowiec but are unable to find a place to hide, as they are turned away by Richieu's former governess. Eventually, they are able to hide at Anja's father's former home. For a time, they live with a woman named Mrs. Kawka, who lets them stay in her barn.

Needing a more permanent place to stay, they come to stay with a woman named Mrs. Motonowa. Although she charges them to live there, it is a better option than the barn. When news comes that the Nazis are coming to search her home, she forces them to leave. After spending the night in a construction site, they return to Mrs. Kawka's barn, and she tells them of a group of smugglers who can transport them to Hungary.

While getting things from the black market, Vladek sees Mrs. Motonowa, who regrets making them leave and invites them to return. After they return to her home, her husband returns from a trip, unaware of their presence, and they are forced to hide in the basement for several days surrounded by rats. Vladek decides that the situation is not safe and that they should meet the smugglers. He is spotted on his way to meet them by a group of Polish children who scream and run away, calling him a Jew. Left with a dilemma, Vladek confronts the parents and assures them that he is a loyal German, which saves his life.

At the meeting are an old acquaintance of Vladek's, Mandelbaum, and his nephew, Abraham. They listen to the smugglers' plans and then discuss it amongst themselves in Yiddish, so that they will not be understood. Everyone feels uncomfortable about the plan, which does not sound safe. Abraham volunteers to go and will send a letter once he arrives safely. Everyone else will wait to travel until after the letter arrives. Although Anja and Mrs. Motonowa don't like the plan, Vladek decides that it is the best available option.

When a letter arrives from Abraham confirming that he has arrived safely, Vladek, Anja, and Mandelbaum meet the smugglers at a train station. Shortly after boarding the train, they are betrayed by the smugglers and are arrested by the Nazis. Vladek and Anja are separated and sent to different camps.

Art asks his father about Anja's diaries, and is told by his father that he destroyed them because the contents made him too sad. Art asks what was in the diaries and is told that Anja wrote that she wished that someday her son would read them. Angered by the news, Art calls his father a murderer.

ESSENTIAL QUESTIONS

1. In this chapter, Vladek says that he can pass as a member of the Gestapo but that his wife is clearly Jewish. How does Art Spiegelman depict this?
2. When the Polish children see Vladek, they seem terrified. How do the stories that the Polish parents tell the children, as well as the ones that German parents tell their children, help facilitate Hitler's Final Solution?
3. The chapter ends with an angry Art calling his father a murderer. When else does he call someone a murderer? Is he justified in doing this or is he being controlled by his emotions?

BOOK 2: AND HERE MY TROUBLES BEGAN

Part I: Mauschwitz

While on vacation in Vermont, Art finds himself conflicted as to how to portray his wife, who is French but converted to Judaism, in the novel. He is approached by a frantic friend who tells him that he received a phone call saying that his father had a heart attack. When he calls back, he learns from his father that he did not have a heart attack but said it so that his son would actually call. The real emergency is that Mala has left him, taking money with her.

Art and Françoise travel to the Catskills where Vladek is staying, and on the trip, Art shares with his wife his conflicted feelings about his father's story. He wishes that he could have seen his parents in the camps to fully understand their experiences. He feels guilty for the easy life that he has had and about his "ghost brother," whom he has only known through photographs, and the rivalry that he feels with him.

When they arrive late at Vladek's bungalow, Vladek gets up to greet them and shares the story of a fight over money at the bank that led Mala to leave him and go to Florida. He is considering pressing charges against her. Art helps his father go over his financial papers. As the stress of the situation begins to get to everyone, Françoise suggests that Art and Vladek go for a walk while she goes over the work. As they walk, Vladek resumes his story.

Once at Auschwitz, Vladek has his clothes taken from him and his head shaved. He is given a cold shower but is grateful that it is not a gas chamber. He is later given a tattoo on the inside of his left forearm. The camp smells of burning rubber and fat and the ominous smokestacks are in the distance.

Vladek sees Mandelbaum and Abraham and discovers that the smugglers forced Abraham to write the letter saying that he had arrived safely. While everyone struggles, Mandelbaum has an especially difficult time, as he has been given ill-fitting clothing.

When Vladek is able to gain favor with a Polish supervisor, the Kapo, by tutoring him in English, he is given access to food and better clothing and is able to take clothing to Mandelbaum. Although excited, Mandelbaum is taken away to work and is never seen again. After tutoring the Kapo for 2 months, Vladek is told that he has been reassigned.

ESSENTIAL QUESTIONS

1. Why is Art so conflicted about how to portray his wife, and what does he settle on?
2. How has the way that Richieu been preserved as "perfect" through photographs and memories been unfair to Art's life?
3. Despite ending up in Auschwitz, how has Vladek been very fortunate up to this point?

Part 2: Auschwitz: Time Flies

Art is attempting to work on the book but is portrayed as a human wearing a mouse mask. As his frustration with the book grows, it is revealed that his desk sits atop a pile of dead Jews from the camps. Feeling overwhelmed with interview requests and marketing ideas, Art visits his psychiatrist, Pavel, who is also a survivor of the Holocaust. When he does, he regresses to a child, and both men are depicted as being human but wearing mouse masks. They discuss the meaning of survival and Art's feelings of guilt.

After leaving his therapy session, Art reverts back to being an adult and seems to feel better. Returning home, he listens to tapes of his father's interviews, including an argument with his father.

Working now in a tin shop, even though he has no experience, Vladek is struggling with the work. The tin shop supervisor, a communist named Yidl, recognizes that Vladek doesn't know what he's doing and despises him for being a former factory owner. Fearing that he'll be transferred, Vladek is able to bribe the supervisor. Meanwhile, supplies are running short and the brutality of the guards is increasing.

While Vladek is in Auschwitz, a work camp, Anja is in Birkenau, which is nothing more than a waiting area before the prisoners are sent to the gas chambers. Using another woman in the camp who is having an affair with a SS officer, Vladek and Anja are able to stay in contact. She is weak and contemplating suicide. She is given jobs that she cannot perform and then beaten when she fails.

Vladek is able to get transferred to Birkenau to be with Anja. However, his time is short when he is caught talking to her by one of the guards, and after he is severely beaten, he finds himself back at Auschwitz.

Sent back to the tin shop and still fearing Yidl, Vladek manages to get transferred to be a shoemaker, something he does know a little about from his time working as a shoe repairman. The high quality of his work puts him in demand, and he is able to get food. Back at Birkenau, Anja is still being beaten regularly. When she notices that the Kapo's shoes are falling apart, she suggests that he send them to Vladek. When the shoes are returned good as new, she is treated better.

By saving all of the gifts he was given for his shoe repairs, Vladek is able to bribe the guards to have Anja transferred. He attempts to give her food but is caught by a guard, and Anja is forced to hide in one of the barracks. A furious guard makes the prisoners exercise until they are exhausted. Eventually, Vladek loses his job near his wife and is forced to do manual labor.

After the Russians invade Poland, the Nazis begin to disassemble the camp, and Vladek returns to work disassembling the gas chambers because of his experience working in the tin shop.

Art wonders why the Jews didn't try to resist and is told that they were all tired and still in disbelief about what was happening. They survived on hope that the Russians would liberate the camp.

ESSENTIAL QUESTIONS

1. At the beginning of the chapter, Art is portrayed as a human wearing a mouse mask. Why did Spiegelman make the choice to portray himself in this manner?

2. When visiting his psychiatrist, he shrinks to the size of a child, and both of them go through the session wearing the mouse masks. Why?

3. Why is it important for Vladek to let Art know that he helped dismantle the ovens and gas chambers? What does it say about him that he considers this important?

Part 3: And Here My Troubles Began

In the morning, Vladek is packing the food that Mala left behind, and credits his refusal to waste anything to his Holocaust experience. When he offers some of the food to Art, who refuses, he becomes angry.

On their trip to the store, Art attempts to ask his father about a story of some of the Jews who attempted to revolt. Art confirms that although the men were successful in killing a few of the Nazis, they were later executed, as were the girls who supplied the ammunition.

The Russians are very close to the camp and the sounds of their artillery can be heard in the distance. Word spreads that the Nazis plan to move everyone in the camp, and Vladek and several other prisoners concoct a plan to hide until the camp is cleared and then escape. He begins to acquire civilian clothes for himself and his coconspirators, but the plan is abandoned when they hear a rumor that the Nazis plan to bomb and burn the camp before it is evacuated; however, the rumor was a hoax and the camp is never actually bombed.

During the move to the train, a long march through the snow, several men attempt to escape and are shot for their efforts. On the trains, the men are starving and are given no food. Vladek is able to reach through a window and retrieve some snow from the top of the car, which he uses to survive. One man has sugar and eats it even though it burns his throat. He asks Vladek to get him some snow, which Vladek does in exchange for sugar.

Only about 25 men survive, and when the train is stopped, the Nazis force the men to throw the bodies from the train. With each stop, the train empties more and more. At one stop, they are surprised to find the Red Cross waiting and are supplied with coffee and bread before reboarding the train.

Once they arrive at the grocery store in present day, Françoise and Art stay in the car out of embarrassment while Vladek returns some partially eaten food for a refund that he had purchased from the same store. From inside the car, they can see him arguing with the store manager. When he returns, he is boastful about getting the money back and says that the manager was very nice about it after learning that he had survived the Holocaust and was recently left by his wife.

WATCH

There have been several very good films made about the Holocaust and the experiences of the survivors. View clips from *The Boy in the Striped Pajamas* (Heyman & Herman, 2008), *Life Is Beautiful* (Braschi, Ferri, & Benigni, 1997), *The Pianist* (Benmussa, Polanski, & Sarde, 2002), and *Schindler's List* (Lustig, Molen, & Spielberg, 1993).

DISCUSS

Make note of and discuss the experiences of the characters in each of the films. What similarities do you notice about the characters? How do these experiences compare to those of Vladek and Anja in *Maus*?

Vladek resumes his story. The train finally arrives at Dachau, which has no gas chambers but is extremely crowded. Each night, the men have to remove their shirt, which is inspected for lice. If the shirt has lice, they receive no food. Vladek aggravates a cut on his hand so that he may be moved to the infirmary, where he receives his own bed and three meals a day. He comes to befriend a Frenchman who is also in the barracks. The Frenchman is able to receive packages, which the Jews cannot. Vladek is able to trade various items that he's collected for a clean shirt, which he wears each night to inspections.

A few weeks later, Vladek contracts typhus, which has spread through the camp. He is transferred again to the infirmary. Although very sick, he continues saving his food to use for bribes. Eventually, he is transferred in an exchange of prisoners of war. He is able to bribe some of the prisoners to help him to the train that will take him to Switzerland.

As Vladek, Art, and Françoise return from the store in the present day, Vladek says that he stayed in contact with the Frenchman for years but burned the letters along with Anja's diaries. Françoise stops and picks up an African American hitchhiker, which agitates Vladek, who sits and mutters to himself in Polish. After they drop off the hitchhiker, Vladek is angry because when he first arrived in New York, he felt that the Blacks in the city would steal his belongings if they were left unattended, and it forever altered how he saw all African Americans.

ESSENTIAL QUESTIONS

1. What is the irony of this chapter?
2. How is Vladek's reaction to the hitchhiker surprising? How does this act in stark contrast to the theme of the book?

Part 4: Saved

The following autumn, Art again visits his father at home. Vladek is clearly lonely and is beginning to question the decisions he's made, placing the value of money above that of his wife. He attempts to get Art to live with him, which Art declines. Art asks his father how Anja survived the war, but his memories of her story aren't as good. He knows that she was marched for a long period and released near Russia before making her way back to Sosnowiec. He launches back into his own story.

Vladek is loaded onto a passenger train that had seats, in stark contrast to the cattle cars that he had traveled in previously and is also given a package of food from the Red Cross. Before the passengers arrive at their destination, they are forced off of the train and marched until they reach another train that will take them to the Americans. When that train is stopped a short time later, they are released, but there are no Americans. The passengers walk off into the distance and wander for awhile before encountering a German patrol. They are marched to a lake and wait through the night anticipating their execution. When morning comes, the Germans are gone, having left their guns. They are eventually picked up by another patrol and again marched to a barn and spend another night anticipating death, only to again discover the Germans gone in the morning.

They come to an abandoned house and stay there for a week, living off of the food in the house. They are eventually rescued by the Americans, who treat them with kindness and feed them.

The chapter ends with Vladek sharing old family photos with Art and sharing stories about the people in them.

ESSENTIAL QUESTIONS

Although only appearing briefly at the end of the chapter, how does Vladek view the American soldiers? How is their characterization important and what does it say about them?

Part 5: The Second Honeymoon

Art is concerned about how to handle his father's deteriorating health. He flies to Florida to visit him and finds that he is in bad shape but is back with Mala. She seems very unhappy and is unsure why she took him back, as he has only gotten more difficult to deal with as his health worsens. Before they all return to New York, Vladek tells Art about his postwar years, telling him that he started out in a labor job before using his skills to work his way up with a Jewish-owned department store.

Upon their return to New York, Art again visits his father to record the final chapter of the book.

After staying with the Americans for awhile, Vladek returns to Poland and begins to search for word of Anja's fate. He finds that she is still alive and living in Sosnowiec, which is still dangerous, and reports come that Poles are still killing Jews. Determined, he writes her a letter and travels to Sosnowiec to find her. They are eventually reunited.

With that, Vladek tells Art that he is finished talking and calls him Richieu, the name of his long-deceased brother.

ESSENTIAL QUESTIONS

1. What is the meaning behind this chapter's title, "The Second Honeymoon"?
2. What is Art's reasoning for having his father call him Richieu? What significance does this hold for him?

ESSAY TOPICS

1. Published toward the end of World War II, George Orwell's (1945/1996) *Animal Farm* thematically shares many of the same ideas as *Maus*. Look at both works and compare the use of allegory to tell stories of oppression. How are the pigs in Orwell's novel similar to the cats in Spiegelman's? How does each use different animals to convey different meanings?

PROJECT

HISTORY THROUGH YOUR FAMILY

Interview a family member about a significant moment in history that occurred during their lifetime. How did it affect them personally? How have their feelings changed about it over time? Use the lines below to brainstorm.

Using the interview, write and illustrate a short, personal story about your family member's life during that moment in history, but portray the characters as animals. Think about which animals you choose and explain why you chose them.

If you don't want to use a family member, try seeking out another adult (e.g., a teacher, a friend of the family, a neighbor, etc.) to interview.

_____

_____

_____

_____

_____

_____

_____

_____

_____

_____

_____

_____

_____

_____

_____

_____

THE TEENAGE EXPERIENCE

In his poem "My Heart Leaps Up," William Wordsworth (1807/2008) presented the paradox "the child is father of the man," meaning who we are in our youth helps define who we will be as adults, and that man is the outcome of the child. Life is an often difficult journey, with the teenage years potentially being the most trying.

The teenage years are often some of the most challenging. Although you are still a child in many regards, the expectations placed on you by adults increases. Some students take on enormous workloads at school while working late hours at their afterschool jobs. Many of their hardships are internal battles. They face peer pressure from their friends to do things they are not yet ready to experience. They are often either left without any resources to deal with their problems or are reluctant to seek out what resources are available to them.

Although many movies and songs delve into the experiences and feelings of teenagers, teenagers in graphic literature were primarily relegated to the role of superhero sidekick, so unless you could empathize with the trials and tribulations of Robin, Speedy, or Wonder Girl, you were woefully underrepresented in graphic literature. That has changed drastically in recent years, as a new crop of books have been released that focus on teenagers. Whether it is about the superhero world, video games, or first loves, graphic literature has finally caught up with movies and music in recognizing that the life of a teenager is a compelling subject.

GHOST WORLD

Originally serialized in creator Daniel Clowes' own comic magazine, *Eightball*, *Ghost World* (2011) began life as single chapters presented in eight issues spanning from June 1993 until March 1997, before it was finally collected into a single edition. The novel tells the story of Enid Coleslaw and her best friend, Rebecca Doppelmeyer, two cynical yet witty and intelligent girls who have recently graduated high school and are navigating the post-high school world of their unnamed hometown.

Themes

Similar to many novels about adolescence, the major theme of *Ghost World* is alienation. The novel's two protagonists, Enid and Rebecca, are adrift in a post-high school world and live their lives without direction. Enid has considerable antisocial tendencies, many of which Rebecca does not share. Rebecca lives with her elderly grandmother and serves as her caretaker but has aspirations for a social life and mainstream acceptance. That, coupled with her attractiveness, causes a rift between her and Enid that runs throughout the book. The two search for meaning in their nameless hometown but are only able to attach themselves to brief obsessions instead of anything meaningful. It is in this quiet desperation that Enid seems to be ultimately doomed.

Characters

Enid Coleslaw: An 18-year-old recent high school graduate, Enid is antisocial and feels directionless in life. She is intelligent but bitter and cynical and seems to take little interest in life, which results in her failing to follow through on anything she sets out to do. Her disinterest often comes across as being heartless or flippant.

Rebecca Doppelmeyer: Although she is Enid's best friend, Rebecca does not share many of Enid's antisocial tendencies and is portrayed as having more mainstream interests. Despite being best friends, Enid characterizes Rebecca as being the embodiment of what every guy wants and is somewhat resentful of her for it. Rebecca lives with her grandmother, for whom she acts as a caretaker.

Chapter 1: Ghost World

We are introduced to Enid and Rebecca as Enid visits Rebecca at home. While there, Enid is annoyed to discover that Rebecca has been reading a trendy teen magazine. As the two watch television together, Enid's underlying resentment of her best friend becomes more apparent as she points out that Rebecca is attractive and could have any guy she wants.

Enid relates to Rebecca a story from the previous day when she was at a local diner with a classmate, John, who brought along a rather uncomfortable-looking older man who sweated profusely. John told Enid that the man, who would not make eye contact with her, is an ex-Catholic priest. While sitting in their booth, Enid noticed a rather strange-looking couple that she called Satanists, and with whom she becomes very fascinated.

LISTEN AND DISCUSS

Singer Aimee Mann's (2000) song "Ghost World" was inspired by the graphic novel. Listen to the song and discuss its connections to the book.

ESSENTIAL QUESTIONS

1. Explain Enid's annoyance at Rebecca for reading a trendy teen magazine. Why does she feel betrayed? Is she justified in having these feelings or she just being rude?
2. Why is Enid's characterization of the couple at the diner as being Satanists ironic?

Chapter 2: Garage Sale

The next day, Enid is holding a yard sale, where she seemingly refuses to sell anything. A customer inquires about a toy that she identifies as "Goofie Gus." When Rebecca asks her why she is having the sale if she won't sell anything, Enid gets annoyed, and the two leave to go look for the Satanist couple.

At the diner, they do not see the couple but do run into a former classmate, whom neither wants to speak to. They leave and go to a nearby grocery store and run into the couple, and Rebecca seems to be just as fascinated with the couple as Enid is.

ESSENTIAL QUESTION

Is it normal behavior for Enid and Rebecca to be so fascinated in the "Satanist couple" or is their behavior a violation of society's norms?

Chapter 3: Punk Day

Enid has cut her hair into a short, punk style. Rebecca arrives and acts horrified to see her new haircut. Enid is angry that her father let Rebecca into the house, but they eventually leave together again to wander the streets. While out, they encounter a bald girl with an enormous growth on her neck. The girl says hi to them, but they don't know who she is. After she leaves looking hurt, Enid realizes that she is a former classmate who has cancer.

That night in Enid's room, Enid finds a business card for a psychic named Bob Skeetes, whom Enid has become obsessed with. They call and leave a message on his phone implying that they are "on to him." Later, the two lament that boys don't find them attractive. Enid jokingly suggests that they become a lesbian couple, which makes Rebecca upset.

ESSENTIAL QUESTIONS

Enid does not hold interest in any one thing for a very long time, and Bob Skeetes seems to have replaced the Satanist couple as her latest obsession. To what do you attribute her brief fascinations with people?

Chapter 4: The First Time

The next evening, Enid calls Rebecca to talk about her day. She forced her classmate Josh, whom Enid is attracted to but will not admit it, into going with her an adult store. The object of the trip, for Enid, seems to be to embarrass Josh, which she succeeds at. They then try to guess whether Josh is or is not a virgin, and Enid shares the story of losing her virginity.

ESSENTIAL QUESTIONS

Why is Enid unable to admit an attraction to Josh but instead ridicules and embarrasses him?

Chapter 5: Hubba Hubba

While at a 1950s-themed diner called Hubba Hubba, Enid and Rebecca look through the local newspaper's "missed connections" section and decide to prank a man who wrote to a woman he met on the bus. They set up a date for him with the mystery woman but feel bad when he shows up and eventually leaves when the woman never arrives.

ESSENTIAL QUESTION

What pleasure do Enid and Rebecca get out of making a fool out of the man they found in the missed connections section?

Chapter 6: The Norman Square

While walking around town, Enid and Rebecca's sadness becomes more and more apparent. They see Mrs. Satanist and attempt to talk to her but walk away when the woman looks confused. As they sit together at a busstop, Enid vows to never go to college. The two had been holding hands, but when Rebecca notices, she immediately tells her to stop.

ESSENTIAL QUESTION

For the second time in the novel, Rebecca becomes uncomfortable at what she perceives as sexual advances made by Enid. Do you interpret Enid's feelings for Rebecca to be romantic or is Enid simply looking for a human connection?

When she is upset in this chapter, Enid retreats to her room and cries while listening to music. Listening to music can be a very emotional experience. What songs do you listen to when you are upset? Does it help?

Chapter 7: A Smile and a Ribbon

Later they look through old photographs from when they were children before deciding to visit Josh, who is not home. While at a diner together, Enid and Rebecca get into a fight because Rebecca feels like she puts everything into their friendship but doesn't get anything in return from Enid. When Enid returns home, her father attempts to be sympathetic, but she gets frustrated and retreats to her room. Feeling hurt and upset, she retreats to her room and cries in bed while listening to music.

Chapter 8: October

Enid and Rebecca have a heart-to-heart, and Rebecca wonders aloud if she is perhaps gay. Enid tells Rebecca of her plan to leave their hometown, and Rebecca feels hurt when she perceives that Enid wouldn't want her to go with her.

When Enid returns home, she finds her father sitting with a woman that he dated when Enid was very young and whom Enid did not like. As the novel concludes, Enid has packed her bags and is leaving on a bus.

ESSENTIAL QUESTIONS

1. Enid clearly does not like her father's girlfriend. Are her feelings of betrayal at her father reuniting with a woman she does not like justified or misguided?

2. At the novel's conclusion, Enid packs her bags and gets on a bus to leave town. Although some have interpreted this move as an easy solution for the character, it can also be viewed as her rejection of the status quo, as she decides to be the master of her own destiny. How do you view Enid's departure at the end of the novel?

3. Many people have attempted to ascertain the meaning behind the title *Ghost World*. What evidence do you see in the novel of its intended meaning? Explain your answer.

PROJECT

MY OWN PERSONAL GHOST WORLD

Throughout the novel, Enid is portrayed as being antisocial and very much detached from the town in which she lives. However, her feelings of alienation are not uncommon among most teenagers. Write a story about a time in your life that you felt lost in the world. Did you overcome it? What did you do to overcome it? What friends and family made the time easier? Which ones made it harder? Include illustrations or pictures to accompany different sections of the story. Use the lines below for brainstorming.

_____

_____

_____

_____

_____

_____

_____

_____

_____

_____

_____

_____

_____

_____

_____

_____

_____

_____

AMERICAN BORN CHINESE

Inspired by a Chinese folktale about a Monkey King, *American Born Chinese* (Yang, 2008), which presents three intertwining stories, was created by Gene Luen Yang, an Oakland, CA, high school computer science teacher. In addition to creating numerous graphic novels, Yang is an advocate for using graphic novels in the classroom for all subjects—not just English. Yang has created an online comic to teach his various concepts to his math students called Factoring With Mr. Yang and Mosley (http://www.geneyang.com/factoring). *American Born Chinese*, his second book following 2004's *Animal Crackers* has become one of the most popular graphic novels to teach.

The novel switches between three different narratives that are tied together as one story in the novel's conclusion. The first story is of the Monkey King and was inspired by the famous Chinese novel *Journey to the West* (Wu, 1592/2003), The second story is about Jin Wang, the son of second-generation Chinese Americans, who has recently moved from a predominately Chinese neighborhood to an all-White neighborhood. The third story is about a White high school student named Danny, whose life is regularly ruined by the annual visit from his Chinese cousin, Chin-Kee, who is the embodiment of every Chinese stereotype.

Themes

The novel has intertwining themes of racial stereotypes and racial identity. The characters in the three different narratives all struggle with how they wish to be perceived by their peers. The Monkey King is rejected by the other deities for being a monkey, which brings forth his anger toward them, but also anger at himself for being who he is. Jin Wang struggles to be accepted at his all-White new school. Danny's social acceptance by his classmates is threatened by the appearance of his cousin, Chin-Kee.

All of the characters face racial stereotypes in their quest for racial identity. It is the Monkey King's rejection by the other deities for being a monkey that leads him on his quest to no longer be a monkey. Similarly, Jin Wang desperately wants to be accepted by his classmates, who mock him by using racial stereotypes, such as implying that he eats dogs and calling him "bucktooth" (p. 34). His fear of these stereotypes makes him initially avoid the friendship of Wei-Chen, who is not ashamed of who he is. In Danny's story, his cousin, Chen-Kee, fits all stereotypes of Chinese-Americans, both good and bad.

Characters

The Monkey King: A deity who is determined to overcome the perception that he's only a monkey. After being slighted at a party in Heaven, he fights all of the other deities who were in attendance at the party. He then returns home and begins arduous meditation and training regiments to no longer be a monkey. He eventually learns a lesson and accepts his identity as a monkey.

Tze-Yo-Tzuh: The creator of the world.

Wong Lai-Tsao: A monk traveling to Tze-Yo-Tzuh. He takes the Monkey King as his disciple.

Jin Wang: A Chinese-American boy who desperately wants to fit in with the white students at his new school. He is initially shy and reserved but receives encouragement from Wei-Chen Sun.

Wei-Chen Sun: A new student to Jin Wang's school after immigrating from Taiwan. He befriends Jin and becomes his only friend. Wei-Chen's true identity is revealed later in the book.

Danny: A White American boy. He is embarrassed when his cousin, Chin-Kee, comes for his annual visit. Danny switches schools every year because of the problems that Chin-Kee causes for him.

Chin-Kee: Danny's Chinese cousin. He embodies many stereotypes of Chinese-Americans. He is loud and speaks broken English and dresses in old-fashioned Chinese clothing, but is also a very good student and incredibly intelligent.

The Monkey King, Part 1

One night all of the gods, goddesses, and demons gathered for a party in Heaven. When the Monkey King arrives, he is denied entrance to the party because he is a monkey. He attempts to argue with the guard and explain that he is a god and deserves entrance. The guard again turns him away by explaining that he cannot come in because he is a monkey. Angered that he is denied entrance, the Monkey King enters the party by force and assaults everyone in attendance, leaving everyone beaten and unconscious. He returns to his home on Flower-Fruit Mountain and notices the thick smell of monkey fur in his home and sits alone in the dark trying to figure out how to rid himself of it.

RESEARCH AND DISCUSS

The Monkey King story is based on *A Journey to the West* (Wu, 1592/2003). Research the story and compare and contrast the depictions of the character in each.

ESSENTIAL QUESTION

After being turned away, the Monkey King reacts in anger and then shame. Are his extreme reactions to his rejection natural?

Jin Wang, Part 1:

Jin Wang tells the story of how his parents, both Chinese immigrants in America, met and fell in love. He was raised in Chinatown in San Francisco, where he had many friends. On a visit to an herbalist, Jin explains to the elderly woman that his toy is a Transformer and that he wishes he could be a Transformer. The woman explains to Jin that he can be anything he wants, as long as he is willing to exchange his soul.

When his family moves, Jin starts school at an all-White school, where he is quickly isolated from his classmates. When the kids do interact with him, it is when he is being bullied and subjected to racist stereotypes. After several months, a new student comes to the school, Wei-Chen Sun, who has recently immigrated from Taiwan with his family. He seeks out Jin's friendship, only to find himself rebuffed. Eventually, Jin accepts his friendship and the two new friends bond over their mutual love of Transformers.

Jin Wang is a fan of Transformer toys, and they play an important role in the story. How do the toys foreshadow future events in the story?

ESSENTIAL QUESTION

Why does Jin Wang initially ignore Wei-Chen's attempts at friendship?

Danny, Part 1:

Danny, a blonde-haired high school student, is studying with a girl, Melanie, whom he obviously has a crush on. Their study session is interrupted by the appearance of Danny's cousin from China, Chin-Kee, who fits many different negative stereotypes of Chinese-Americans. His loud presence embarrasses Danny in front of the girl.

ESSENTIAL QUESTION

How does the author use sitcom conventions to show how mass media shapes our perceptions of ethnic identity?

The Monkey King, Part 2

The Monkey King has secluded himself to train alone. He spends 40 days training to master the four major invulnerabilities to fire, cold, drowning, and wounds. Once he has mastered them, he spends another 40 days mastering the four disciplines of form: giant, miniature, hair-into-clones, and shape-shifting.

Emerging from his seclusion and looking more like a man than a monkey, the Monkey King receives a death sentence from Heaven for trespassing. He goes and visits each of the gods, goddesses, and demons who have condemned him. He finds that again they laugh at him, so he attacks each of them. He soon meets Tze-Yo-Tzuh, the creator of the heavens, who tells him that he cannot escape his grasp. The Monkey King flees to prove that he can and comes upon the Five Golden Pillars, which he desecrates. When the Monkey King returns to boast that he escaped his grasp, the creator holds up his hand, which bears the same marking the Monkey King put on one of the pillars. The Monkey King maintains his superiority, and in response to his arrogance, he is buried under a mountain of stones, where he remains trapped.

Discuss

The Monkey King focuses his efforts on becoming invincible and shape-shifting. If he wanted to be superior, what are other things the Monkey could have trained for?

ESSENTIAL QUESTIONS

1. The Monkey King spends a great amount of time in seclusion as he masters several disciplines. When he confronts the same people who had turned him away at the party in heaven, he demonstrates his superiority by again fighting them. What is his error in logic in using the same approach?

2. The Five Golden Pillars turn out to be the fingers of Tze-Yo-Tzuh. Why are his fingers a symbol of truth?

Write & Illustrate

Jin changes his hair to look more like what he considers to be normal. Write a short personal essay about a time that you attempted to change in some way to be more accepted. Add illustrations of your "transformation."

Jin Wang, Part 2

In school, Jin has developed a crush on a girl named Amelia. He later sees her talking to a boy with curly, blonde hair, and he becomes jealous. Wei-Chen, who has a girlfriend, notices and encourages Jin to talk to Amelia. As they talk, they overhear two male students make racist jokes about Asians. The next day, Jin arrives at school with his hair styled like the boy Amelia was talking to the previous day. When Amelia and Wei-Chen accidentally are locked together in a closet in their science class, Wei-Chen reveals to Amelia that Jin has a crush on her. When Jin arrives and lets them out, Wei-Chen convinces him to ask her out, to which she says yes.

Danny, Part 2

Chin-Kee has started attending classes with Danny, where he proves to be highly intelligent and overzealous, a positive stereotype. At lunch the same day, he is seen eating cooked cat meat and then plays a prank on Danny's friend by urinating in his soda, both negative stereotypes. When Danny finally is able to talk to Melanie for the first time since Chin-Kee's arrival, she is kind. As the two are talking, she notices that Danny has buck teeth and gives him the card for her orthodontist.

In the gym, Danny talks to his friend, Steve, about his feelings about Chin-Kee visiting every year since eighth grade, which always ruins his reputation and forces him to move. His friend assures him that the students at school aren't like that and to not worry. When Danny reveals the joke that Chin-Kee played on the friend, it makes him sick.

The Monkey King, Part 3

The chapter begins with the story of a monk who attempts to achieve legendary status. When he is unable to achieve the status through meditation, he is awarded it when his love and kindness is recognized by Tze-Yo-Tzuh. He is sent on a quest and promised three disciples, one of which is the Monkey King. The monk finds the Monkey King and explains that he is to be the monk's disciple. The Monkey King, still imprisoned under the rock, is insulted and refuses to go. When the monk is attacked in front of him by two demons, the Monkey King admits his stubbornness and reverts back to his true form of a small monkey and is able to free himself. He then fends off the demon and frees the monk, agreeing to become his disciple.

ESSENTIAL QUESTIONS

1. The story begins with the story of three different monks who achieve legendary status through meditation, fasting, and sermons. The fourth monk, though, is unable to excel at any of those three things. However, he achieves legendary status through his love and kindness. What statement is being made about humility and good deeds?

2. The Monkey King has remained imprisoned under a large pile of stones for a long time. He is able but unwilling to free himself. What is truly imprisoning him?

The Monkey King is finally freed from his prison by admitting that he was stubborn. Describe a time that you were stubborn and what it took for you to admit that you were wrong.

Jin Wang, Part 3

Jin finally goes on a date with Amelia to the movies after lying to his mother about where he's going and making Wei-Chen cover for him. During the date, he realizes that he has body odor, which makes him self-conscious. He asks Wei-Chen to talk to Amelia the next day to see if she noticed. During their conversation, Amelia tells him that she had a great time on her date with Jin and that nothing went wrong. Initially excited, Jin daydreams about being with Amelia forever. His dream is ruined when the blonde-haired boy with the hairstyle he's been mimicking approaches him and asks him to not see Amelia again because he wants her to make good choices.

Feeling sad and dejected, he talks to Wei-Chen's girlfriend, Suzy, who opens up to Jin about feeling rejected by her oldest friend. She begins to cry during the story, and Jin responds by kissing her. She is angered by this and hits him. When Wei-Chen confronts him, Jin is rude and insults his only friend, who responds by hitting him. That night when he goes to bed, he dreams of the herbalist who told him how he could be a transformer. She asks him in the dream what he would like to become. When he awakens in the night, he goes to the bathroom and discovers, after looking in the mirror, that he is Danny from the third story.

The end of the chapter reveals that Jin is actually Danny from the third story. What evidence did you see throughout the story that hinted at this revelation?

ESSENTIAL QUESTION

Why did Jin refuse to stand up for himself when the boy asked him to stop seeing Amelia?

Danny, Part 3

After witnessing Chin-Kee singing in the library, an embarrassed Danny fights him. Their fight carries on for some time with Chin-Kee holding the advantage for most of it. At the end of their fight, Danny punches Chin-Kee and knocks his head off, revealing that he is the Monkey King in disguise.

The Monkey King tells Danny that it is time that he reveals his true form as well, and Danny reverts back to being Jin Wang. The Monkey King explains that he is an emissary of Tze-Yo-Tzuh and that he sent his only son to Earth as Wei-Chen to pursue a mission of living vice-free for 40 years. Wei-Chen had to give up his mission after lying to Jin's mother to help Jin go on his date.

When his son abandoned the mission, the Monkey King began to visit Jin in disguise as Chin-Kee to serve as a guidepost to his soul. He tells Jin that he must atone for his mistakes and make peace with Wei-Chen.

The two meet later at a diner, and Jin apologizes to Wei-Chen. The story concludes with the two as friends once again.

It's revealed at the end of the story that Chin-Kee and Wei-Chen were actually the Monkey King and his son. Why did the author portray Chin-Kee as such a broad stereotype of Chinese people?

ESSENTIAL QUESTIONS

1. Each story is told in a different manner, with the Monkey King's story being told as traditional folk tale and the Danny and Chin-Kee story being told like a sitcom. Why did the author choose each style for the particular story?
2. What lessons did the Monkey King pass along to Jin Wang?
3. What is the importance of names to the character's identities?
4. How does the story of the Monkey King serve as an allegory for the story of Jin Wang?

PROJECT

MY LIFE AS A FABLE

The genesis for *American Born Chinese* was the fable of the Monkey King. Gene Yang took a well-known Chinese fable and used it as part of a story of a young boy struggling with his own identity in an environment that doesn't readily accept him for who he is. Using Yang's idea as inspiration, research a famous fable and create a short graphic story about yourself using the fable to make a point about who you are and where you come from. In addition, create a reflection about the project, including why you chose the fable and how you personally identified with its protagonist. Use the lines below for making notes or brainstorming.

_____

_____

_____

_____

_____

_____

_____

_____

_____

_____

_____

_____

_____

_____

_____

_____

_____

_____

CHAPTER 9

MAKING YOUR OWN GRAPHIC NOVEL

SUGGESTED TIMELINE 3–4 WEEKS

Note: This project can be done as a stand-alone unit or as an ongoing project throughout the semester or year. The suggested timeline below approaches the project as a stand-alone unit.

- The story (1–2 weeks)
  - Elements of plot (1 day)
  - Plotting the story (1 day)
  - Character biographies (1–2 days)
  - The script (4–5 days)
- The art (2 weeks)
  - Photo referencing for practice/layout language (2–3 days)
  - Pencils/Inking (3–4 days)
  - Lettering (2–3 days)
  - Coloring (2–3 days)
- Presentation of graphic novels to class (2–3 days)

As I'm sure many kids did upon reading his or her first comic book, I immediately attempted to write my own, and indeed I did. I turned out numerous awful Spider-Man stories that were each essentially a poorly drawn and terribly written rip-off of an issue that I had recently read. The greatest expanses that my creativity could reach amounted to switching the characters around from various stories or making hybrid characters, such as my vastly underappreciated original creations Super-Spider and Captain Batman.

My mother, kind as she is, assured me that each of them was wonderful and creative. If you care to view any of them, they are all currently available in the Ryan J. Novak museum, which is housed in a filing cabinet in her laundry room along with school pictures and badly written short stories and poems from high school.

What I was too young to understand then and wouldn't fully grasp until I took several writing courses in college was that the first failure of my writing was that I wasn't writing for me, I was simply regurgitating what I had already seen. It's the difference between hearing someone who is genuinely funny versus someone who is telling a mediocre joke that was heard secondhand—one makes a lasting impression and the other is easily forgotten.

HAVE A STORY TO TELL

Through my early attempts at writing a comic book when I was a kid or movies, plays, and short stories when I was a teenager, I regularly missed one thing: the story. I had ideas for cool things, like big fights or chase scenes, but the story that led to those moments was often weak. Without a strong story, the reader will lose interest. The story doesn't have to include fights, explosions, and chases to be engaging. Regardless of what type of story or genre a student wants to write, he or she must, at the heart, have a strong story. To start, a good story needs to include all five elements of plot. Explore with students the five elements of plot and what each entails.

Elements of Plot

Exposition. The exposition is the establishment of the story. During the exposition, the reader learns the setting and many of the central characters. It serves to establish the basis of a story on which the plot is built.

Rising Action. This is when the story is established, and the main conflict is revealed to the reader. By now, the reader will have a firm grasp on who the characters are, and what the story is.

Climax. The highest point of emotion or tension in the story occurs during the climax. Often, people mistake the end of the story for the climax, which is not the case. Think of a favorite movie or story and pick out the climax.

Falling Action. Following the climax, the story begins to rapidly work toward its conclusion. This is the falling action. The falling action features the characters dealing with the fallout of the climax.

Resolution. The resolution brings the story to its conclusion. Whether the end of the story is a definite end or is being used as the set-up for the next chapter, the resolution will still see the plot concluded.

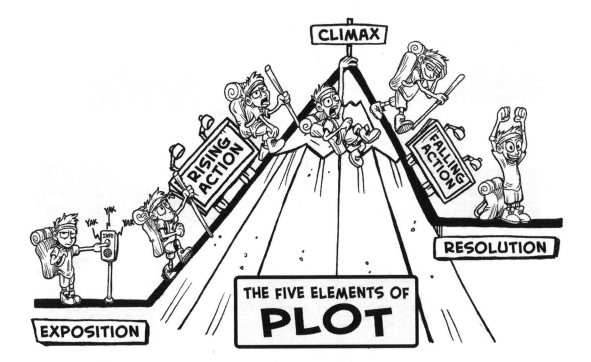

In addition to the elements of plot, every story must include the following:

- **Protagonist:** The protagonist is the main character in the story (e.g., Superman, Batman, or Luke Skywalker).
- **Antagonist:** This is the character or force that opposes the protagonist (e.g., Lex Luthor, the Joker, or Darth Vader).
- **Plot:** The plot is what the story is about.
- **Setting:** The setting is where the story takes place. This is not limited to the physical location (e.g., Boston or outer space), but the time period in which it takes place (e.g., the old West or the not-too-distant future).
- **Conflict:** The central struggle that drives the plot is the conflict. Conflicts can be divided into two categories: internal and external. External conflict includes man versus man, man versus nature, and man versus machine. Internal conflict is man versus himself.
- **Tone:** Tone is the author's attitude toward his or her subject. The tone that the author uses will affect the story's mood.
- **Mood:** The overall feeling or emotion that the story creates for the reader is the mood. A love story, which will usually have a lighter tone, will create a happier mood for the reader. A scary story, which will have a darker tone, will create a gloomy, unsettling mood for the reader.

WATCH AND DISCUSS

Watch the trailer for Disney's *Mary Poppins* on YouTube (http://www. youtube.com/watch?v=fuWf9fP-A-U) and then the reimagined trailer for "Scary Mary" (http://www.youtube.com/watch?v=2T5_OAGdFic). Discuss how subtle changes can alter the mood.

WATCH AND DISCUSS

Watch clips from movies that demonstrate each element of plot, such as *Wizard of Oz* or *Ghostbusters*.

WRITING YOUR STORY

Have you ever started telling a story and realized midway through that it wasn't interesting? Have you ever watched a movie with a plot that seemed to go nowhere? The first thing that a writer needs to decide before beginning the writing process is what story he or she wants to tell. It's important to not think in terms of genre or even characters, but simply what the story is about. Have students start by deciding the basics of the story:

- Who or what is the protagonist?
- Who or what is the antagonist?
- What is the central conflict?
- What is the setting?

Plotting Your Story

Write

- Choose several famous stories in film and literature and distill the story to its most basic elements. Compare the plots to see which stories are similar.
- Review the four types of conflict and find a story that features each conflict.

Now that the basics have been established, it's time to start breaking down the plot. First, have students divide a paper into five sections and label them as exposition, rising action, climax, falling action, and resolution. Remember that each scene needs to have one purpose: to move the plot forward. With that in mind, make sure students write under each section which scenes need to be included to move the plot forward. How will they get from the exposition to the rising action? What will take the readers to the climax? What plot twist will take place following the climax to get through the falling action to the resolution? Have students ask themselves with each scene they write how it is helping to move the plot forward.

Character Biography

Brainstorm

What does your character look like? Does he or she look like someone you know? Write down each character in your story and then a person who is similar in look and personality.

In order to write an effective and believable character for the reader, the writer needs to know everything about the character. That's why I recommend that students write bios for all of their major characters (this is sometimes called a "character bible"). Although students will certainly make changes to their characters as they write, the biography will give them a foundation for him or her. Handout 9.1 will help establish some of the basic character elements.

HANDOUT 9.1
CHARACTER BIOGRAPHY

NAME:	
AGE:	
PARENTS:	
SIBLINGS:	
CHILDHOOD:	
CHILDHOOD FRIENDS:	
EDUCATION:	
INTERESTS:	
CHARACTERISTICS:	
JOBS/CAREER:	
CLOTHING STYLE:	
ROMANTIC HISTORY:	

CHARACTER BIOGRAPHY, CONTINUED

BEST FRIEND:
WORST ENEMY:
LIFE GOAL:
TALENT:
GREATEST FEAR:
CHARACTER'S FAVORITES
COLOR:
MUSIC:
MOVIES:
BOOKS:

THE SCRIPT

The importance of the script is often overlooked. Just like a movie script, a graphic novel script details exactly how the finished product will look. If the author is both the writer and the artist, the script may not need to be as detailed as it would if there were a separate illustrator. In any case, the artist needs detailed instructions on how the page needs to be filled.

Formatting Your Script

At the top of a blank page, have students put the page number and number of panels for that page. It's best to not exceed six panels per page in order to have room to effectively tell the story in each panel. When a new character is introduced, his or her name needs to be in all caps and followed by a description of that character. Have students begin each new page of their story on a new page in their script.

For each panel, write what is taking place in that panel with any dialogue written underneath it. A sample script is provided on the next page.

SAMPLE SCRIPT

Panel 1

A large group of birds (you decide the number) are taking flight

Narrator:

Being able to fly like a bird is a dream of many

Panel 2:

A young boy (modeled however you want) stands with his hands on his hips in his best Superman pose. He is wearing pajamas with a blanket tied around his neck, like a cape.

Narrator:

As children, we all dreamed of it

Panel 3:

A frog sits on the ground stairing up at birds taking flight. He looks sad

Narrator:

But humans are not the only ones who have this dream.

Panel 4:

The frog daydreams of being able to fly. His thought balloon has an image of him taking flight with birds wings sprouting from his back.

Panel 5:

The frog now looks happy.

Frog:

I'm gonna fly like the birds!

Panel 6:

A group of birds are standing nearby and overhear him.

Bird 1:

You're a frog, stupid! Frogs can't fly!

Other birds:

Hahahaha!

Panel 7:

The frog again looks sad

Frog (sadly):

I'll prove them wrong

Script Shorthand

When writing a script, a writer needs to communicate exactly what he or she wants the artist to do, so the writer will need as much space as possible for the descriptions. By using some shorthand terms, there will be more space available for the script. In order to save some time and space on the script, I recommend that students use the following shorthand terms:

- OP: indicates that action or dialogue is taking place off panel;
- Sound Effects (SFX): indicates a sound effect that is meant for the reader to "hear;"
- Cap: indicates that the words should be written as a caption
- Whisper: indicating that the words should be written as a whisper;
- Thought: indicates that the words should be written in a thought balloon;
- Close up: indicates that the panel will be filled by only one person or item;
- Point of View (POV): something is seen from the perspective of a character;
- Exterior (EXT.): anything that takes place outside;
- Interior (INT.): anything that takes place inside;
- Flashback: action that is inserted out-of-sequence in the story, such as a character remembering something; and
- Cut to/Transition: anytime there is a change in action from one location to another.

Dialogue

The voice of each character needs to be as unique as the characters themselves. It helps to base a character on someone the storyteller knows, whether it's a friend, family member, or acquaintance. When students have settled on a voice for each character, make sure they consistently try to stick to it.

Have students read the dialogue out loud as they write it. Do the words hold true to the character they've established, or are they simply there to take up space? If it doesn't sound like something the character would actually say, then have the students change it because the reader will notice, just as they did.

Advise students to keep your ears open for dialogue. Have you ever listened to a conversation between two people and heard something funny or interesting? Maybe you followed the entire conversation or heard it out of context, but was it still stuck in your head? Give some examples to students, and then have them practice active listening during lunch or free time in other classes. Have them write down what they hear so they can refer back to it as they write their story dialogue.

ART

For many students, the art is perhaps the most intimidating part of creating a graphic novel, but it doesn't need to be. Students simply need to find their own style. Have them refer back to their character biographies and decide what each character looks like. Once they've settled on an appearance, they can draw each character expressing every emotion that they can imagine as initial practice (e.g., happy, sad, mad, tired, scared, nervous, sick, lonely, hot, cold, confused, frustrated, etc.).

Photo Referencing

One good method for learning to illustrate is to take pictures. Have students use a camera or a phone to take photo reference pictures. Have them refer back to their script and see what they need for every panel. Have them try to recreate those panels in real life—they can ask a family member to model different facial expressions and reactions, or they can capture scenery or locations that they can use in their story. If students don't have access to a camera, they can research images online or use books from the library.

Students don't have to be intimidated by drawing. Have them draw what they see in the pictures they've taken or researched, but they should do it lightly with a pencil at first. Using a pencil, they can carefully make changes to the art as they refine each panel to be exactly what they want it to be. A rough sketch and a refined sketch are presented as examples below.

Layout Language

Below is a basic panel. Students should remember that a panel can be what they need it to be. It can be any size or shape, and doesn't have to be the standard quadrilateral panel below. Its function is to move the story forward.

As discussed, dialogue is important to the story. The dialogue balloons are just as important to the reader in order to understand the dialogue.

Just as every person doesn't speak at the same volume all day, the characters will not either. Dialogue balloons should reflect this.

Sometimes characters speak in normal conversational tones.

Sometimes characters yell!

Sometimes they whisper...

And sometimes they keep their thoughts to themselves.

Basic Layouts

Just as we read left to right, so too must the action take place—after all, it is called "sequential art." Make sure students do not overwhelm the page with panels or the panel itself with too much action or dialogue. The story itself takes precedent, so have them spread the words and action out as much as their story needs to be effectively told. It helps to think of a story like a movie and include changes in perspective and angle. It will help keep the reader's interest.

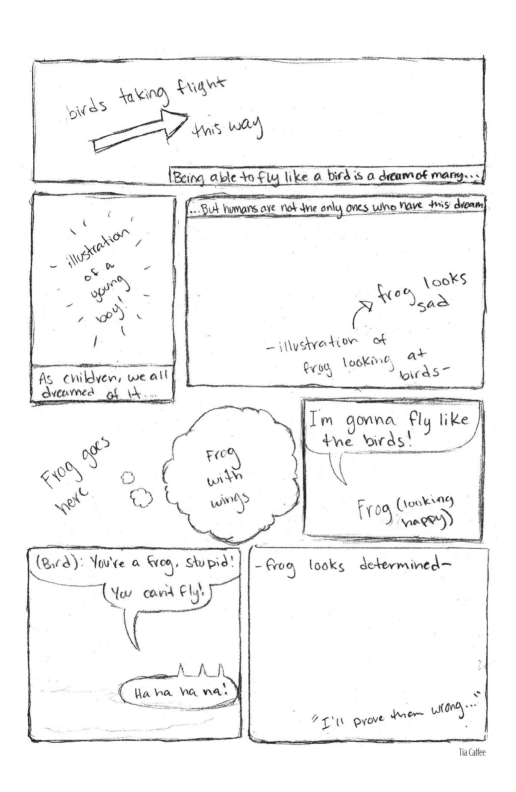

Tia Calfee

This is what a basic layout will look like. Let students know it's okay to use stick figures because at this stage they are only settling on what they want each panel to look like.

Tia Calfee

The Pencils

These are the finished pencils drawn from the preceding page. I've included a portion of the script on p. 140 so you can see the transformation from script to finished pencils.

Tia Calfee

Inking

There are three different types of lines when putting the finished inks on a page: thin, thick, and scratchy. Have students pick the type of line that will work the best for their story, but encourage them to vary in style as they find necessary.

The thin line is smooth and consistent and is the kind used in most superhero stories.

The thick line is more consistent for an animated or cartoon style drawing.

The scratchy line is one synonymous with showing action (or you may associate it with Charles Schulz' "Peanuts" comics).

Lettering

If a student has clean, easy-to-read handwriting, then encourage him or her to letter by hand the captions and dialogue. However, if a student is like me, and his or her handwriting is a little on the inconsistent side, then he or she might prefer to use a typed font for the lettering. The advantage to using a font from a computer is that students can change the font to dictate a certain mood for a scene or even to make a distinction between different characters.

Coloring

Although a story can be told in black and white and be perfectly effective, many students may want to color their story. If this is the case, have them look back at their photo references for inspiration. The grass is green, the sky is blue, and the sun is yellow most of the time, but is it always? Encourage students explore different possibilities. How does the grass look in an area that hasn't gotten much rainfall? How does the sky look as the sun sets? How does the sun look early in the morning or late in the afternoon? Have students experiment (on pages separate from their panels) with different colors and shades.

FINISHED PAGE

Below is an example of the finished page developed throughout the chapter. We've gone from a script to a rough sketch, to a penciled drawing, to an inked page, and finally to the finished, colored page. Just as this page has developed, so too will your students' stories. By taking their graphic novel one step at a time, they will arrive at a finished product that fits their vision. Good luck and have fun!

Tia Calfee

CONCLUSION

When I was just learning to read, I learned by reading comic books that my grandfather would buy me on our trips to the grocery store. Granddad would always joke that I shouldn't let my grandmother know because she would throw a fit—which she did, telling him that they were a waste of time and that I shouldn't be learning to read from "picture books." Although her heart was in the right place, the thing she missed about those "picture books" was that the art didn't detract from the story but enhanced it.

The art in a comic book or graphic novel serves a number of purposes. It advances the story when there is no dialogue to do so. It adds another layer to the story and presents the world as the writer/artist views it. Finally, it expands the imagination of the reader.

For me, as I'm sure it was for many people who learned to read with comic books, the importance of the third item is immeasurable. Like many children, I had a vivid imagination, but comic books expanded the possibilities of it. Although *Star Wars* and Indiana Jones certainly did their fair share in helping shape my childhood world of adventure and excitement, comic books took it to the stratosphere. I could invest myself completely in the world of Spider-Man because Peter Parker was an awkward kid like me, albeit with superpowers. I could identify with Batman because he was a superhero without any superpowers.

Now that I'm a teacher and am frequently encountering students who are apprehensive about reading, I reflect back on my childhood and how the books that I was given in school did little to grab my attention—they were given to me for no other reason than that they were "grade-level appropriate." It was graphic literature that was truly captured my imagination. Although some may fail to see the connection, the alienation that Peter Parker felt as an awkward teenager with superpowers was not all that different from the same feelings of alienation that J.D. Salinger's (1951/1991) classic character, Holden Caulfield, felt at the series of private schools he was carted off to by his parents in *The Catcher in the Rye*. Even though they are delivered in different forms, both characters are timeless.

With graphic literature, I found myself and a love of reading at the same time, which is what I have found to be the consensus among the students who I have had in class who also share a passion for the format. Graphic literature allows readers to enter new worlds and immerse themselves fully. We see the world, not solely as we imagine it to be, but as the writer and artist want it to be. It is in those strange new worlds, however, that we may find ourselves.

REFERENCES

Albert, T. (Producer), & Norrington, S. (Director). (2003). *The league of extraordinary gentlemen* [Motion picture]. United States: Angry Films.

Alighieri, D. (2013). *The divine comedy*. New York, NY: Simon & Brown. (Original work written c. 1308)

Andre, F., Kahn, G., & Schwandt, W. (1968). Dream a little dream of me [Recorded by The Mamas & The Papas]. On *The Papas & The Mamas* [Record]. New York, NY: Dunhill.

Arad, A., Tolmach, M., & Ziskin, L. (Producers), & Webb, M. (Director). (2012). *The amazing Spider-Man* [Motion picture]. United States: Columbia Pictures, Marvel Entertainment, & Laura Ziskin Productions.

Ballard, P. (1954). Mister sandman [Recorded by The Chordettes]. On *Mister sandman* single [Record]. New York, NY: Cadence.

Benmussa, R., Polanski, R., & Sarde, A. (Producers), & Polanski, R. (Director). (2002). *The pianist* [Motion picture]. France and Poland: R. P. Productions and Heritage Films.

Braschi, G., & Ferri, E. (Producers), & Benigni, R. (Director). (1997). *Life is beautiful* [Motion picture]. Italy: Cecchi Gori Pictures.

Bryant, F., & Bryant, B. (1958). All I have to do is dream [Recorded by The Everly Brothers]. On *All I have to do is dream* single [Record]. New York, NY: Cadence.

Clowes, D. (2001). *Ghost world*. Seattle, WA: Fantagraphics.

Doyle, A. C. (2012). *The adventure of the final problem.* London, England: Solis Press. (Original work published in 1893)

Dylan, B. (1968). All along the watchtower. On *John Wesley Harding* [Record]. New York, NY: Columbia. (1967)

Eisner, W. (2006). *A contract with God.* New York, NY: Norton. (Original work published in 1978)

Eliot, T. S. (2000). *The waste land.* New York, NY: Norton. (Original work published in 1922)

Fiege, K. (Producer), & Whedon, J. (Director). (2012). *The avengers* [Motion picture]. United States: Marvel Studios and Paramount Pictures.

Frank, A. (1993). *The diary of a young girl.* New York, NY: Bantam. (Original work published in 1947)

Gaiman, N. (2004, February 2). Snow day [Blog post]. Retrieved from http://journal.neilgaiman.com/2004/02/snow-day.asp

Gaiman, N. (2012a, May). *Make good art.* Keynote address presented at the 134th commencement of The University of the Arts, Philadelphia, PA. Retrieved from http://www.uarts.edu/neil-gaiman-keynote-address-2012

Gaiman, N. (2012b). *Sandman* [10 volume set]. New York, NY: Vertigo.

Goodman, G., Kinberg, S., Shuler Donner, L., & Singer, B. (Producers), & Vaughn, M. (Director). (2011). *X-Men: First class* [Motion picture]. United States: Twentieth Century Fox.

Green, J. (2009). *Binky Brown meets the Holy Virgin Mary.* San Francisco, CA: McSweeney's. (Original work published in 1972)

Grimm, J., & Grimm, W. (2011). *Grimm's complete fairy tales.* London, England: Canterbury Classics. (Original work published in 1812)

Haggard, H. R. (2008). *King Solomon's mines.* New York, NY: Penguin. (Original work published in 1885)

Hawks, H. (Producer), & Nyby, C. (Director). (1951). *The thing from another world* [Motion picture]. United States: Winchester Pictures.

Heyman, D. (Producer), & Herman, M. (Director). (2008). *The boy in the striped pajamas* [Motion picture]. United Kingdom: Miramax.

Huxley, A. (2006). *Brave new world.* New York, NY: HarperCollins. (Original work published in 1932)

Katzman, S. (Producer), & Bennet, S. G. (Director). (1950). *Atom Man vs. Superman* [Motion picture]. United States: Columbia Picures.

Kubert, J. (2011). *Yossel.* New York, NY: Vertigo.

Lennox, A., & Stewart, D. A. (1983). Sweet dreams (are made of this) [Recorded by Eurythmics]. On *Sweet dreams (are made of this)* [Record]. New York, NY: RCA. (1982)

Lustig, B., Molen, G., & Spielberg, S. (Producers), & Spielberg, S. (Director). (1993). *Schindler's list* [Motion picture]. United States: Universal Pictures.

Mann, A. (2000). Ghost world. On *Bachelor No. 2* [CD]. Los Angeles, CA: SuperEgo Records.

Miller, F. (1997). *The Dark Knight returns*. New York, NY: DC Comics.

Miller, F. (1999). *300*. Milwaukie, OR: Dark Horse Comics.

Miller, F. (2004). *The Dark Knight strikes again*. New York, NY: DC Comics.

Miller, F. (2005). *Sin city*. Milwaukie, OR: Dark Horse Comics.

Milton, J. (2005). *Paradise lost*. Mineola, NY: Dover. (Original work published in 1667)

Moore, A. (1995). *Watchmen*. New York, NY: DC Comics.

Moore, A. (2000). *From hell*. Marietta, GA: Top Shelf Productions.

Moore, A. (2002). *The league of extraordinary gentlemen: Vol. 1*. New York, NY: America's Best Comics.

Moore, A.(2008a). *Batman: The killing joke*. New York, NY: DC Comics.

Moore, A. (2008b). *V for vendetta*. New York, NY: Vertigo.

Orbison, R. (1963). In dreams. On *In dreams* [Record]. Washington, DC: Monument.

Orwell, G. (1983). *1984*. New York, NY: Plume. (Original work published in 1949)

Orwell, G. (1996). *Animal farm*. New York, NY: Signet. (Original work published in 1945)

Pekar, H. (2003). *American splendor and more American splendor: The life and times of Harvey Pekar*. New York, NY: Ballantine.

Plato. (2007). *The republic*. New York, NY: Penguin. (Original work written c. 380 BCE)

Rohmer, S. (2012). *The mystery of Dr. Fu Manchu*. London, England: Titan. (Original work published in 1913)

Salinger, J. D. (1991). *The catcher in the rye*. New York, NY: Little, Brown. (Original work published in 1951)

Satrapi, M. (2004). *Persepolis: The Story of a childhood*. New York, NY: Pantheon.

Selman, M. (Writer), & Kruse, N. (Director). (2007). Husbands and knives [Television series episode]. In A. Jean (Executive producer), *The Simpsons*. New York, NY: Fox Broadcasting.

Senate Committee on the Judiciary. (1954). *Comic books and juvenile delinquency interim report of the committee on the judiciary pursuant to S. Res. 89 and S. Res. 190: A part of the investigation of juvenile delinquency in the United States*. Retrieved from http://www.thecomicbooks.com/1955senateinterim.html

Shakespeare, W. (1991). *Julius Caesar*. Mineola, NY: Dover. (Original work written c. 1599)

Shakespeare, W. (1998). *Macbeth*. New York, NY: Signet. (Original work written c. 1603)

Shakespeare, W. (2009). *A midsummer night's dream*. Oxford, England: Oxford University Press. (Original work written c. 1590)

Shelley, P. B. (2002). Ozymandias. In D. Reiman & N. Fraistat (Eds.), *Shelley's poetry and prose* (p. 109). New York, NY: Norton. (Original work published in 1818)

Smith, J. (2004). *Bone: The complete cartoon epic in one volume.* Columbus, OH: Cartoon Books.

Sophocles. (1991). *Oedipus Rex.* Mineola, NY: Dover. (Original work written c. 429 BCE)

Spiegelman, A. (1996). *Maus: A survivor's tale.* New York, NY: Pantheon.

Spiegelman, A. (2004). *In the shadow of no towers.* New York, NY: Pantheon.

Stevenson, R. L. (1991). *Strange case of Dr. Jekyll and Mr. Hyde.* Mineola, NY: Dover. (Original work published in 1886)

Stoker, B. (2000). *Dracula.* Mineola, NY: Dover. (Original work published in 1897)

Tan, S. (2007). *The arrival.* New York, NY: Arthur A. Levine Books.

Tezuka, O. (2003). *Metropolis.* Milwaukie, OR: Dark Horse Comics. (Original work published in 1949)

Tezuka, O. (2008). *Astro boy: Vol. 1 & 2.* Milwaukie, OR: Dark Horse Comics.

Thompson, C. (2003). *Blankets.* Marietta, GA: Top Shelf Productions.

Verne, J. (1988). *The mysterious island.* New York, NY: Scribner. (Original work published in 1874)

Verne, J. (2006). *20,000 leagues under the sea.* Mineola, NY: Dover. (Original work published in 1870)

Ware, C. (2003). *Jimmy Corrigan: The smartest kid on Earth.* New York, NY: Pantheon.

Wells, H. G. (2000). *The first men in the moon.* Mineola, NY: Dover. (Original work published in 1901)

Wells, H. G. (2012). *The invisible man.* New York, NY: Simon & Brown. (Original work published in 1897)

Wertham, F. (1954). *Seduction of the innocent.* New York, NY: Rinehart & Company.

Wordsworth, W. (2008). My heart leaps up. In S. Gill (Ed.), *William Wordsworth: The major works* (p. 246). Oxford, England: Oxford University Press. (Original work published in 1807)

Wu, C. (2003). *Journey to the West.* Beijing, China: Foreign Languages Press. (Original work written c. 1592)

Yang, G. L. (2008). *American born Chinese.* New York, NY: Square Fish.

SUGGESTED READING

Although I gave a lot of consideration to which books would best represent each genre discussed, I know that many well-deserving books did not make the final cut. Many of the choices were difficult to make and several books were left out for no reason other than available space. In order to rectify this, I've included a list of very worthy books in each genre that would have otherwise made the cut.

SUPERHEROES
- *Kingdom Come* by Mark Waid
- *Marvels* by Kurt Busiek
- *Cla$$war* by Rob Williams

FANTASY
- *Bone: Out of Boneville* by Jeff Smith
- *Cerebus: High Society* by Dave Sim

SCIENCE FICTION
- *Y: The Last Man* by Brian K. Vaughan
- *Walking Dead: Days Gone By* by Robert Kirkman

MANGA
- *Akira, Vol. 1* by Katsuhiro Otomo
- *Astro Boy, Vol. 1* by Osamu Tezuka

FICTION
- *Box Office Poison* by Alex Robinson
- *Jimmy Corrigan, the Smartest Kid on Earth* by Chris Ware

BIOGRAPHY/MEMOIR
- *Persepolis* by Marjane Satrapi
- *American Splendor: The Life and Times of Harvey Pekar* by Harvey Pekar

THE TEENAGE EXPERIENCE
- *Blankets* by Craig Thompson
- *Scott Pilgrim's Precious Little Life* by Bryan Lee O'Malley

FILM GUIDE

Several films were mentioned throughout the chapters (all readily available by means of Netflix or other streaming sites). Included here are films that are also recommended but were not listed.

HISTORY OF THE MEDIUM
- *Look, Up in the Sky! The Amazing Story of Superman*, directed by Kevin Burns
- *With Great Power: The Stan Lee Story*, directed by Terry Douglas, Nikki Frakes, and Will Hess

SUPERHEROES
- *Batman*, directed by Tim Burton
- *Superman*, directed by Richard Donner
- *The Avengers*, directed by Joss Whedon

FANTASY
- *Coraline*, directed by Henry Selick
- *The Mirror Mask*, directed by James Fotopoulos

SCIENCE FICTION
- *Fahrenheit 451* directed by François Truffaut
- *Hunger Games* directed by Gary Ross
- *THX 1138* directed by George Lucas

MANGA
- *Spirited Away* directed by Hayao Miyazaki
- *Akira* directed by Katsuhiro Ohtomo
- *Howl's Moving Castle* directed by Hayao Miyazaki

FICTION
- *The League of Extraordinary Gentlemen* directed by Stephen Norrington

BIOGRAPHY/MEMOIR
- *American Splendor* directed by Shari Springer Berman and Robert Pulcini
- *An American Tail* directed by Don Bluth
- *Persepolis* directed by Vincent Paronnaud and Marjane Satrapi

THE TEENAGE EXPERIENCE
- *Scott Pilgrim vs. the World* directed by Edgar Wright
- *Breakfast Club* directed by John Hughes
- *Ghost World* directed by Terry Zwigoff

GRAPHIC NOVEL RUBRIC

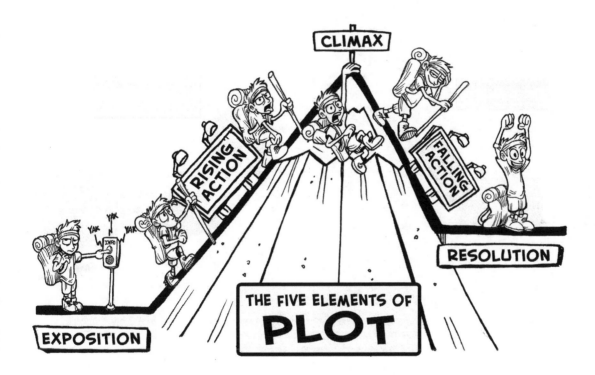

GRAPHIC NOVEL RUBRIC

	4	3	2	1
Story	The story is clear, well organized and easy to read. Important narrative aspects such as the climax and resolution are very clear. The reader finishes the story feeling it is complete and no major details are missing.	The story is clear and well organized, but there are one or two points of confusion. Important narrative aspects such as the climax and resolution are clear. The reader finishes the story feeling it is complete and no major details are missing.	The story is sometimes clear, but disorganized. Important narrative aspects such as the climax and resolution are not completely clear. The reader finishes the story feeling it is complete but that major details are missing.	The story is confused and unclear. Important narrative aspects such as the climax and resolution are missing. The narrative is difficult to read because it is so disjointed. The reader finishes the story feeling it is incomplete.
Word Choice	Strong, descriptive language is used and all captions are concise.	Most language is clear and concise and for the most part strong and descriptive.	The language is inconsistent, strong at times but often weak others.	The language is overly simple and not at all descriptive.
Panel Layout	Panels are designed in a way that greatly enhances the overall visual effect. The design and layout clearly enhance the artwork and text.	Panels are designed in a way that for the most part enhances the overall visual effect. The design and layout enhance the artwork and text, but there are one or two instances where the layout detracts from the story.	Panels are designed in a way that adds to the overall visual effect for about half of the graphic novel. The design and layout often enhance the artwork and text, but there are multiple instances where the layout detracts from the story.	Panels lack design and do not enhance the overall visual effect. The design and layout do not enhance the artwork and text.
Images	All Images are striking and powerful. All images enhance the story and work seamlessly with the text. All images are high quality, clear, and are not pixelated. All of the images are original or of a student's own creative remixing or adaptation.	Most images are striking and powerful and add to the meaning of the text. Most images are high quality, clear, and are not pixelated. Most of the images are original or of a student's own creative remixing or adaptation.	There are some striking and powerful images, but some are dull and don't lend meaning to the text. Some images enhance the story, but some images detract from the story because they are confusing, of low quality, unclear, and/or pixelated. Some images seem to be completely lifted or are reminiscent of something else.	Very few images are striking or powerful, and many seem boring and unrelated. Images rarely enhance the story, and most images detract from the story because they are confusing, of low quality, unclear, and/or pixelated. Most of the images seem to be lifted or are reminiscent of something else.
Attention to Detail	There are no distracting errors, corrections, or erasures, and the novel is easily read. There are no errors in grammar, spelling, or punctuation.	There are only one or two distracting errors, corrections, or erasures. There are minor errors in grammar, spelling, or punctuation.	Fairly readable, but the quality is not very good on some parts. It looks like the student ran out of time. There are several errors in grammar, spelling, or punctuation.	Very messy and hard to read. It looks like it was put together at the last minute without much care. There are excessive errors in spelling, grammar, or punctuation.

ABOUT THE AUTHOR

Ryan J. Novak teaches dual-credit English and mythology in Dixon, MO. His love of graphic literature began in childhood when he learned to read using comic books that his grandfather bought for him at the supermarket. His interest in teaching it as literature came from sponsoring a comic book club and noticing how his students responded to different genres of graphic literature. He lives in Springfield, MO, with his wife, Lindsey.

Teaching Graphic Novels in the Classroom

All lessons in this book align to the following standards.

Grade Level	Common Core State Standards in ELA-Literacy
Grade 7	RL7.1: Cite several pieces of textual evidence to support analysis of what the text says explicitly as well as inferences drawn from the text. RL7.2: Determine a theme or central idea of a text and analyze its development over the course of the text; provide an objective summary of the text. RL.7.3: Analyze how particular elements of a story or drama interact (e.g., how setting shapes the characters or plot). RL.7.4: Determine the meaning of words and phrases as they are used in a text, including figurative and connotative meanings; analyze the impact of rhymes and other repetitions of sounds (e.g., alliteration) on a specific verse or stanza of a poem or section of a story or drama. RL.7.5: Analyze how a drama's or poem's form or structure (e.g., soliloquy, sonnet) contributes to its meaning RL.7.6: Analyze how an author develops and contrasts the points of view of different characters or narrators in a text.
Grade 8	RL.8.1: Cite the textual evidence that most strongly supports an analysis of what the text says explicitly as well as inferences drawn from the text. RL.8.2: Determine a theme or central idea of a text and analyze its development over the course of the text, including its relationship to the characters, setting, and plot; provide an objective summary of the text. RL.8.3: Analyze how particular lines of dialogue or incidents in a story or drama propel the action, reveal aspects of a character, or provoke a decision. RL.8.4: Determine the meaning of words and phrases as they are used in a text, including figurative and connotative meanings; analyze the impact of specific word choices on meaning and tone, including analogies or allusions to other texts. RL.8.5: Compare and contrast the structure of two or more texts and analyze how the differing structure of each text contributes to its meaning and style. RL.8.6: Analyze how differences in the points of view of the characters and the audience or reader (e.g., created through the use of dramatic irony) create such effects as suspense or humor.
Grades 9-10	RL.9-10.1: Cite strong and thorough textual evidence to support analysis of what the text says explicitly as well as inferences drawn from the text. RL.9-10.2: Determine a theme or central idea of a text and analyze in detail its development over the course of the text, including how it emerges and is shaped and refined by specific details; provide an objective summary of the text. RL.9-10.3: Analyze how complex characters (e.g., those with multiple or conflicting motivations) develop over the course of a text, interact with other characters, and advance the plot or develop the theme. RL.9-10.4: Determine the meaning of words and phrases as they are used in the text, including figurative and connotative meanings; analyze the cumulative impact of specific word choices on meaning and tone (e.g., how the language evokes a sense of time and place; how it sets a formal or informal tone). RL.9-10.5: Analyze how an author's choices concerning how to structure a text, order events within it (e.g., parallel plots), and manipulate time (e.g., pacing, flashbacks) create such effects as mystery, tension, or surprise. W.9-10.6: Analyze a particular point of view or cultural experience reflected in a work of literature from outside the United States, drawing on a wide reading of world literature.
Grades 11-12	RL.11-12.1: Cite strong and thorough textual evidence to support analysis of what the text says explicitly as well as inferences drawn from the text, including determining where the text leaves matters uncertain. RL.11-12.2: Determine two or more themes or central ideas of a text and analyze their development over the course of the text, including how they interact and build on one another to produce a complex account; provide an objective summary of the text. RL.11-12.3: Analyze the impact of the author's choices regarding how to develop and relate elements of a story or drama (e.g., where a story is set, how the action is ordered, how the characters are introduced and developed). RL.11-12.4: Determine the meaning of words and phrases as they are used in the text, including figurative and connotative meanings; analyze the impact of specific word choices on meaning and tone, including words with multiple meanings or language that is particularly fresh, engaging, or beautiful. (Include Shakespeare as well as other authors.) RL.11-12.5: Analyze how an author's choices concerning how to structure specific parts of a text (e.g., the choice of where to begin or end a story, the choice to provide a comedic or tragic resolution) contribute to its overall structure and meaning as well as its aesthetic impact. RL.11-12.6: Analyze a case in which grasping a point of view requires distinguishing what is directly stated in a text from what is really meant (e.g., satire, sarcasm, irony, or understatement).